D1123465

5@55

THE 5 ESSENTIAL LEGAL DOCUMENTS YOU NEED BY AGE 55

By Judith D. Grimaldi

and

Joanne Seminara

with

Pierre A. Lehu

Quill
Driver
Books

Fresno, California

5@55

Published by Quill Driver Books,
an imprint of Linden Publishing
2006 South Mary, Fresno, California 93721
559-233-6633 / 800-345-4447
QuillDriverBooks.com

Quill Driver Books and Colophon are trademarks
of Linden Publishing, Inc.

DISCLAIMER: This book is intended to inform, not to advise. No one should attempt to interpret or apply any law without the aid of an attorney. This is particularly true of elder law and trusts and estates law. You should consult an attorney of your choice before making decisions in all areas of the law discussed in this book.

ISBN 978-1-61035-258-1

Printed in the United States

First Printing

Library of Congress Cataloging-in-Publication Data

Grimaldi, Judith D., author.
 5@55 : the 5 essential legal documents you need by age 55 / by Judith D. Grimaldi and Joanne Seminara with Pierre A. Lehu.
     pages cm
 Includes index.
 ISBN 978-1-61035-258-1 (pbk. : alk. paper)
 1. Estate planning–United States. I. Seminara, Joanne, author. II. Lehu, Pierre A., author. III. Title. IV. Title: Five at fifty-five.
 KF750.Z9G75 2015
 332.024'0160973–dc23

                    2015011846

Contents

This book is dedicated to our clients. You graciously entrust us with your life stories and we, in turn, are inspired by your kindness and courage.

Foreword

I approach this project—and this extraordinary book—from a relatively unique perspective. For seven years, I was Surrogate Judge in New York County, perhaps the busiest and most litigious court in the nation for battles about the apportioning of estates. And prior to that I served on the court that hears adult guardianship cases, where many of the problems described in this book are unfortunately resolved. At the age of 72, I am also (although not for much longer!) a person who has inexplicably failed to do all of the advanced planning so appropriately encouraged by the authors of *5@55*.

This book discusses in depth the five documents that are critical for advanced planning. Everyone should understand that if someone dies without a Will it is the law, not the person's wishes, that determines distribution of his or her estate. This law, called intestacy, operates according to a very strict hierarchy of persons who would inherit, which is entirely dependent upon *blood* relationships. As such, a person who died without a Will, and also without a living spouse, children, siblings, or parents, would have his or her estate distributed to nieces or nephews, if any, or to first or even second cousins whom the deceased may never have met. Entirely left out could be people such as a cherished stepchild, devoted friend, or beloved domestic partner who had provided years of care and support. I know this because I saw it month after month in my courtroom, and was saddened because I knew these results could not possibly have been the wishes of the deceased. But without a Will, I was powerless to change things. "If only they had planned ahead," I often thought.

In my time as a judge hearing guardianship cases, I also saw the needless expense and affronts to a person's dignity that inevitably accompany a guardianship proceeding. Guardianship all too often removes both liberty and property rights from a person, and robs her or him of the ability to make personal choices over a wide range of issues. A guardianship hearing exposes in excruciating detail all of the weaknesses and inadequacies of the person for whom the guardianship is sought—with him or her present to hear it. This is not an experience any of us would want to go through. All of this can be avoided if a person has made appropriate plans in advance, which may include Powers of Attorney, Trusts, and health care decision-making instruments.

Perhaps most difficult and heartbreaking are the cases in which a court is required to make medical decisions, particularly end-of-life decisions where there is no advance directive. Similar to guardianship proceedings, these often pit children or other relatives against each other with regard to medical decisions that a person ought to be able to make for herself, but which she may now be incapable of either making or communicating. How can we possibly decide who knows best in these situations? And I have seen, as well, the bitterness and guilt of family members who, in the former case have been removed from the decision-making process, and who, in the latter, have made life-ending decisions without any absolute certainty that such decisions were what the person her/himself would have made.

So you would think that I, of all people, would have executed all five documents proposed by the 5@55 project. But, like so many people who will read this book, or whose lawyers will read this book, I haven't. In fact, I've never even thought about my cyber afterlife and what steps I might take to deal with that situation appropriately. I can assure you, however, after reading this thoughtful, perceptive, and legally well-grounded book, I will do so, and I would strongly suggest that you read it and share the authors' wisdom and do so as well.

Kristin Booth Glen, University Professor and Dean Emerita,
CUNY School of Law, Surrogate Judge, NY County (Ret.)

Preface

Our five decades of combined law practice have taught us that receiving early legal planning advice from a qualified attorney about the five basic legal documents described in this book is priceless. Timely planning helps people avoid stress and indecision at critical transitional moments in their lives and can provide loved ones with peace and financial security. We approach the practice of law as compassionate advocates for our clients. We hope that our book presents complicated legal concepts clearly and concisely through the lens of our many years of practice in the fields of elder law, estates and trusts, and special needs law.

As lawyers, we often write more formally. But *5@55* is *not* a tome for lawyers written in "legalese." Our goal is to demystify the estate planning process and simplify the concepts. Our co-author, Pierre A. Lehu, deserves a great deal of credit for making our subject matter more palatable and understandable by helping to write this book in a clear, realistic, and sometimes humorous style.

Through our stories and descriptions, we explain the basic need for the five crucial documents that almost everyone of us should have in place on or before our 55th birthday. Our goal is to persuade you, our reader, to undertake the important task of finding an appropriate lawyer who can help you create these five documents, and thereby protect you, your estate, and your loved ones from the expense and delay that often accompanies the settlement of an estate through an in-court proceeding.

We wrote this book as a result of our clients' experiences in difficult situations which would have been much simpler and less stressful if precautionary planning had been done. Our goal is to give you an inside view of what to do to avoid pre- and post-retirement pitfalls.

This *5@55* book is part of a larger campaign to stop the procrastination and establish 55 as the age by which all of us should have our five basic legal planning documents in order. We are often approached by families when it is too late to create and employ these documents due to advanced illness or incapacity. We now bring these tools and "know how" to the attention of younger people with the goal of reducing family stress and avoiding the mistakes we've seen so many others make.

It is our hope that this legal guide will encourage you to step onto the path to planning your future by learning about and executing the five essential legal documents that can make a positive difference in your life and the lives of those you love. We hope you will experience successful aging and be prepared for the challenges of growing old, fortified with the security that planning can bring.

Joanne Seminara, Esq.
Judith D. Grimaldi, Esq.

Introduction

When we approach age 55, we begin to notice changes in ourselves: how we look at the world, our role in our family, and the importance of our work. We acknowledge that we are moving into a new phase as age and the passage of time become more important factors in our lives. We face the nagging reality that we need to formulate plans, make decisions, look to the future, and start to imagine ourselves retired or in a different setting. We see our families growing, leaving the home nest, spreading out, and multiplying with new generations. Our parents are well into their old age. We may see our partners, spouses, and significant family members aging and needing our help. And our own health may be changing as well.

Yet we push those thoughts aside. We make excuses, and say things such as, "Tomorrow I will deal with it. I will make a plan for my future life and my family's life when I am not so busy, when I really need it, or when I can save some money." We hate to admit that time is marching on and we must change and adapt before it is too late and circumstances prevent us from doing so. That is why 55 is the ideal age to take stock and consciously design a plan to clearly define our wishes and take proper care of our loved ones.

As attorneys who have practiced in the fields of elder law and estate planning for many decades, we have seen many clients who failed to plan ahead. The results were frequently disastrous. As lawyers, we cannot address every conceivable life situation or predict the future, but we can assist with putting your legal house in order. We offer *5@55* as a guide to help you learn about five essential legal tools everyone should have by age 55.

Most people in midlife have insurance policies to protect them financially against the ravages of a fire, flood, auto accident, or serious health crisis. They pay their premiums month after month without giving it a second thought. But when it comes to protecting themselves and their family members with some simple legal documents, they bury their heads in the sand.

As two attorneys who truly empathize with our clients, we decided to see if we could help remedy the situation. This book is part of an educational campaign to inform those members of the public who are 55 or older and who are without the five most basic legal documents of the risks they may incur by failing to plan ahead.

While your house may never catch on fire, or you may never get into a traffic accident, avoiding all the effects of not having these five documents is impossible—because everyone dies eventually. True, you may or may not suffer the consequences, but your family members and friends likely will.

One reason for this is that while the damage caused by a fire or auto accident is quite visible, most people keep their legal and financial problems hidden. The likelihood is that you don't know much of anything about your neighbor's legal problems, and that might even be just as true about those of your family members. So in this book we open up our case files (while always making sure that nobody can be identified) and hope to convince those without the five basic legal documents to get a move on.

By the way, this book is not just for those 55 or over. In fact, if you're under 55 and have parents who are older and not protected, it might be even more important that you read it. Armed with the information in this book, you may be able to convince them to see a lawyer no matter their age, because the older you get, the more imperative it is that you and your estate be protected.

5@55 is written to be easily comprehensible. It's not a law book, but one written for the layperson. We must warn you that the stories inside are a bit scary. They're meant to shock you, or your family members, into action. But the best part is that these situations are all avoidable if you just take the time and effort to plan ahead.

~

CHAPTER ONE

The Importance of Being Prepared

Nobody likes going to the doctor to get pricked by a needle, but to avoid the flu you accept that getting a flu shot is the right step to take. Going to see a lawyer is perhaps no more popular than going to see a doctor. But just as the flu shot can prevent future doctor visits, certain documents that your lawyer recommends function as a "vaccine" against future legal problems for you and your family. This legal vaccine comprises five basic legal documents that can protect you: the Healthcare Proxy, the Living Will, the Power of Attorney, the Will, and the Digital Diary.

WHY CREATE THESE FIVE LEGAL DOCUMENTS?

Just as doctors see a steady stream of sick people all day long, lawyers' offices are filled with people who are tangled up in legal issues. What is frustrating to lawyers is that many of these issues could have been prevented if the proper legal work had been done beforehand. By failing to "inoculate" themselves against common and unavoidable health and end-of-life scenarios through the preparation of the proper legal papers, people find themselves with major legal headaches that often involve costly trips to court to resolve. Here's one common example:

Mom is a widow. She falls ill and requires an extended hospital stay. She has expenses that need to be taken care of, but she is unable to sign checks. Mom has never signed any legal documents allowing family members to act on her behalf. She has savings, but they are out of reach of family members who now must pay her day-to-day living expenses, such as utility bills and real estate taxes, out of their own pockets. If her utilities were shut off in the heart of winter and her pipes were to freeze, her house could suffer severe damage. And not paying her taxes could damage her credit, which over time could lead to foreclosure of her house, or the house being sold at auction for nonpayment of taxes.

This is a simple example of a predictable and avoidable situation. As you will see, most such cases are more complicated. The point is that during a time when family members are undergoing tremendous stress concerning Mom's health, spending much of their free time visiting her in the hospital and having to become medical experts in order to make sure she's getting the best care, they don't need additional burdens. They shouldn't have to scrounge around to find the money—and perhaps even be forced to borrow and pay interest—in order to shoulder Mom's financial responsibilities, especially when monthly checks to pay these expenses are being direct-deposited into her account, an account to which the family has no access. And then there are families where the children don't get along, fights break out, and "complicated" turns into all-out war!

To prevent you or your family from having to navigate a crisis of this type, particularly at a critical moment when you don't need another headache, you should have five basic documents prepared by an attorney: 1. Health Care Proxy (or Advance Directive), 2. Living Will, 3. Power of Attorney, 4. Last Will and Testament, and 5. Electronic Information for the Executor, which we call your "Digital Diary" (a form you should use to record electronic information for use by your executor). These are the "basic five" that make up the legal safety net lawyers advise that you put into place (samples of these documents can be found in the Appendices).

WHY AT AGE 55?

Facing up to the downsides of getting older or having a possible legal crisis is not pleasant. Preparing the five important documents forces you to contemplate the worst of what the future may hold, so it's not surprising that people put it off over and over again. (Statistics show that 60 percent of all adults don't have a Will.) And the need to talk with your family about the future doesn't make it any easier. So while many people know that they should spend the time to create the legal documents that will be needed as they age, they find a million excuses to say "tomorrow."

Now 55 isn't necessarily a magic number. You could certainly have these documents prepared at a younger age. Depending on your exact circumstances, that might be very wise. If you're a soldier going off to an overseas post, you'd want to make sure someone back home could handle financial matters for you. Or maybe you travel for weeks or months at a time for your job. Or have medical conditions that put you at risk for frequent hospitalization. As the then 37-year-old John F. Kennedy noted in his Will, "We must be mindful of the uncertainty of life!"

If you fall into the "I'll get to it eventually" trap, there's a good chance that "eventually" will turn into "never."

So you see there are plenty of reasons to have this paperwork done well before you reach 55. That said, health matters often become more serious with age, while your assets and lifestyle are also more likely to undergo changes.

If you fall into the "I'll get to it eventually" trap, there's a good chance that "eventually" will turn into "never." So by giving yourself a deadline, at some point during the year you turn 55, you'll have the added incentive to actually follow through and get those papers drawn up and signed.

Another reason that 55 is a good age to acquire these documents is that for many people that's an age when their children have reached "legal capacity." That means the children can legally sign documents and are old enough to understand the consequences of these documents. In addition, they are likely to be old enough to be capable of helping in a crisis. If you're married and are involved in an auto accident, for example, there's a good chance your spouse would be in the car, too. That's why making sure your adult children are also in the picture is important. It's even more crucial for single people without children to take advance precautions, as there may be no one who automatically could take on the role of representative for them.

Many parents make a Will when their children are young and legally dependent in order to name a guardian for them if something were to happen to both parents. If you're in that group, undoubtedly much will have changed over the years, so age 55 is certainly a good time to make a new Will and consider other legal needs.

Other reasons make age 55 a milestone in your life. 55 is around the time when your body starts to undergo physical changes that can make becoming ill or facing physical impairments more likely. For example, your body loses the ability to regenerate its DNA at 55, which is why damaged cells heal more slowly and may even be more likely to turn cancerous. And anyone who has reached the age of 55 will start to notice that even minor injuries take longer to heal. The Social Security Administration (SSA) considers 55 to be the point when you are considered to be at an "advanced" age, an age when it will be harder to change your career if you were to lose your current job. That's why 55 is the starting age at which the SSA is more likely to approve disability benefits. If you retire or stop working at age 55, you can also make 401(k)—but not IRA—withdrawals without having to pay a penalty (though you do have to pay the resulting taxes). In addition, statistically the incomes of most Americans tend to decrease starting at age 55.

55 is also the average age recommended to purchase long-term-care insurance, which is special insurance coverage that pays for any long-term care not covered by Medicare or other health insurance. In truth, making sure that you can afford long-term care if you need it should be a part of everyone's retirement plan.

Summing up, events with serious consequences can strike at any time, so protecting yourself and your family with advance planning would be a positive step at any age. But if you still haven't taken action by age 55, make *this* the year you stop procrastinating—because the odds of your needing the protection of these important legal documents are now far too high to ignore.

WHY NOT AT AGE 75?

We've given you the main reasons why age 55 should be the upper age limit when it comes to obtaining these five documents. Yet we know that many people remain unprotected long after they turn 55. So let's look at the other side of this equation. Why is waiting until you pass age 55 a mistake?

First of all, you might not make it to 75. The census proves that people are living longer. But the statistics don't offer you any individual guarantee that you will make it to 75. Yes, you could end up living far longer than the average person, but the older you are, your chances of being at death's door increase. More importantly, by age 75 you've probably experienced one or more health issues. Doctors and modern medicine can and do work miracles, but any time you go under anesthesia, for example, you undergo the risk of not waking up. And sometimes even the best doctors can't cure what ails you.

And then there's the epidemic of Alzheimer's disease. According to the Alzheimer's Association, the number of people who will develop Alzheimer's, or some other form of dementia, in the next twenty years is staggering. While we all hope for a cure, it won't arrive soon enough for tens of millions of Americans. And you or your spouse or partner could be one of them. Alzheimer's, while not an immediate death sentence, causes increasing mental incapacity, which, except in its early stages, renders a person incapable of understanding legal documents. And recent studies have shown that one of the first signs of dementia is the inability to handle mathematical reasoning and therefore finances. In fact, on average, one's ability to make financial decisions peaks at age 53 and begins a slow decline, even in those who never develop dementia. So the longer you wait to face the financial decisions that are part of making a Will and other estate planning paperwork, the more difficult you will find understanding all the possible ramifications.

As you get older, even legal paperwork that is not inherently financial in nature may become more difficult to grasp, and that's especially true if dementia, even in its early stages, is present. If an Alzheimer's sufferer does not have or can no longer execute a durable Power of Attorney (the document we describe in Chapter Four), the results can be financially disastrous due to the high cost of long-term care for persons who suffer this dreaded disease.

Even if Alzheimer's is not a factor, older persons often find it harder to grasp the legal concepts presented by the five documents and may experience anguish about the choices presented to them. We have seen that aging may be accompanied by increased insecurity in dealing with already emotional issues concerning family and finances. We're not psychologists, but the aging process definitely seems to make it harder to reach sound decisions. Time and again we see that even simple legal concept may be difficult for our older senior clients to understand or deal with. A question like, "Who would you like to be the executor of your Will?" posed to an 85-year-old woman may be overwhelming. This is not always an easy question for someone 55 or younger to answer, but the older you get the harder it becomes.

Many times the draft documents we prepare for older clients will be taken home unsigned for them to review and think about. Sometimes, we never see those clients again, or they come in again only after a lot of prodding. Are they poring over the documents, not fully understanding them, or did they simply put them in a drawer and refuse to look at them? We can't know the answer to that question but we see it again and again. Very often, it's their children that push them into making decisions because they see changes in mom or dad and realize that action needs to be taken before matters take a turn for the worse and signing documents becomes impossible.

Making end-of-life decisions can be unpleasant and even difficult at age 55, when death is hopefully far down the road. But as you age, thoughts about your own death may begin to bother you to the extent that you actively push them out of your head and deny the need to plan. In short, it's far better to address the documents presented in this book as soon as you can.

WHY DO YOU NEED A LAWYER?

You've seen the ads on television saying that you can order a Will for a bargain rate from some online company. And there are computer programs that also will kick out a form Will with a few clicks of the mouse. Since you may use software to prepare your taxes, you may ask, why not just use one of these programs for my Will and other legal documents? The simple answer is that if these documents aren't properly prepared, they may end up being worthless. In addition, more often than not legal planning documents need to be individualized to meet your particular needs. It is not enough to just fill in the blanks; you must know the right questions to pose and customize the answers so that they pertain to your specific situation.

If your tax forms are wrong, soon after April 15 you'll hear from the IRS and, like it or not, the IRS will demand that you fix them. But the courts won't examine your Will to see if it will pass muster until you pass away. Of course, at that time it will be too late to fix it so that your loved ones don't suffer the consequences of a Will that is flawed or does not provide the outcome you hoped for. As any lawyer will tell you, the plain vanilla Will almost never fits a given client's needs. Families are complex because the people who make up them are unique individuals with myriad lifestyles. Just as your family members couldn't fit into one-size-fits-all clothing, it's unlikely that they can be covered by one-size-fits-all legal documents.

But even if a Will states your wishes, that doesn't mean that some relative won't decide to contest your Will in court. Your relative could say that the Will should be declared invalid so that he or she can attempt to collect more from your estate than your Will left to them. Even one of our nation's Founding Fathers, George Washington, worried about that. When preparing his own Will, he provided for a panel of three impartial and intelligent men to arbitrate any disputes that might arise. So you see, families have been fighting about these issues since the birth of our country.

When you're sick, you go to a doctor, and hopefully you have health insurance that will pay for all or most of the services you need. There are at least two incentives for you to seek medical care: the obvious immediate need for treatment and cure, as well as the financial backing of your health insurance. Unfortunately, the preparation of legal documents does not offer the same incentives, but instead has what some might consider two disincentives. First, the documents you prepare won't result in immediate benefits, as the actual need for the documents won't occur until some time in the future. And second, you have to pay the full cost of preparing the documents today. So it's understandable that so many people put off getting them.

But therein lies the trap that a large number of people fall into. The unresolved legal problems that lawyers deal with are analogous to the medical problems that doctors encounter in caring for patients who didn't take responsibility for their health and end up sick because of it. Untreated legal issues can easily become horror stories, and even run-of-the-mill problems can cost families thousands of needlessly spent dollars. Hopefully, you won't need the 5@55 legal safety-net documents anytime soon. But no one lives forever and individuals tend to experience more serious ailments as they get older, so you should look at obtaining these crucial documents as an investment in your future.

> **Preparing a Will means thinking about your own death, and that's a subject not everyone feels comfortable dealing with.**

PSYCHOLOGICAL BARRIER

To be honest, a major obstacle to convincing people to see a lawyer about drawing up this type of paperwork is psychological. Preparing a Will means thinking about your own death, and that's a subject not everyone feels comfortable dealing with. But, ironically, that is another good reason to force yourself to take this step at age 55. If you don't, you're only going to get closer to death's door, which is likely to make the process of planning harder to deal with.

At age 55, you have every chance of living another twenty to thirty or more years. Unless you're very ill, you're not staring death in the face. So while it's an unpleasant topic, and one you may have been avoiding, it's far better to address the legal issues raised by this paperwork while death is somewhere off in the distance than around the corner. At 55, you've hopefully arrived at a time of your life where subjects such as death and dementia are not too scary, but are scary enough to give you the impetus to make preparations.

We all know people who've had unexpected misfortunes befall them. Consider family members, friends, and former classmates who are about your age and have already passed away or become seriously disabled. So if you think that you have plenty of time to get this paperwork done, remembering those whose lives were cut short should motivate you to take action.

And as for any financial disincentives you may feel, keep in mind that the cost of legal work, be it preparing paperwork or going to court to repair the damage of not having the proper documents, is only going to increase as the years go by. While today's cost may appear steep, it will look far smaller from the perspective of the future.

HOW DO I FIND A GOOD LAWYER?

If you don't already have a lawyer, the best way to find one is through personal reference. Lawyers who specialize in preparing the 5@55 documents are usually called "elder lawyers," "estate planning lawyers," or "trust and estate specialists," although many general practice lawyers (but not all) may be able to assist you. Ask your family members and friends if they have a lawyer. Undoubtedly some will, and they'll be able to tell you whether or not they've been satisfied with the service they've received. Be aware that not every lawyer is in the business of making these documents. Many attorneys specialize in unrelated areas and may not have the proper experience. But if your cousin had an attorney who did a great job handling a medical malpractice suit and you called up that office, even if they couldn't help you, there's a good chance they'd be able to recommend another firm that could.

CHOOSING AN ELDER LAW OR ESTATE PLANNING LAWYER

Just as you'll get better care for a particular illness from a specialist rather than a GP, the same is true when it comes to lawyers. If you use an experienced elder law or estate planning attorney, you'll be less likely to create the type of problem that Mary did:

Mary always wanted her three children to share her estate equally, so she went to a lawyer and had a Will drawn up that did just that. One of Mary's daughters lived nearby, while her other two daughters lived in other states. As Mary got older her arthritis flared occasionally and she needed more help with certain chores, like going to the bank. So to simplify her life, she put her bank account into a joint account with her daughter who lived close by. Mary thought that her Will would take precedence, but by putting all her savings in a joint account with one daughter, she'd basically removed that money from her estate upon her death. Though the other two daughters tried to fight it, the nearby daughter ended up with all the money.

An experienced elder law attorney would have asked Mary where she kept her assets, how her assets were titled, and what changes need to be made so that the wishes expressed in her Will would be carried out. She could easily have opened a small account to hold jointly with one daughter, leaving the rest of her estate to be shared. Or else she could have put all her assets in a Trust and had the nearby daughter be the trustee. The Trust would have distributed the money equally to all three daughters after Mary's death.

WHAT IS A TRUST?

Although this book focuses primarily on the use of Wills in estate planning, we often recommend a Trust, or one or more Trusts and a Will, in estate planning. So a basic definition of the term "Trust" is in order.

A Trust is a document created to manage assets in which an individual names a trustee who is "entrusted" to handle the assets that are transferred to the Trust. The assets are held in the Trust for the benefit of, or "in trust for," one or more beneficiaries of the Trust. The Trust document tells the trustee how she must manage and "pay out" the Trust assets. A Trust can be a substitute for a Will or used together with a Will. A Trust can be created by you during your lifetime or created by your Will upon your death.

The many different types of Trusts serve different needs. For example, a Trust may be created for long-term care planning. Trusts are also used to avoid probate, for gift and tax planning, to provide for children, grandchildren, and the disabled, or to address a combination of these or other needs.

ELDER LAW AND ESTATE PLANNING ATTORNEYS

Just as doctors specialize, so do attorneys. There are good reasons for this. Our laws are voluminous and complicated and change regularly. No one person can keep track of every single law over the wide scope of topics that law covers. And the law can get so complicated that individual lawyers, as well as entire firms, specialize in particular areas of the law. An experienced legal specialist will be familiar with the laws in which they concentrate their practice.

Rather than being defined by technical and legal distinctions, "elder law" and "special needs law" are defined by the clients to be served. In other words, an attorney who practices elder law or special needs law works primarily with people as they age or people with disabilities, respectively.

Elder law and special needs law attorneys use a variety of legal tools and techniques to meet the goals and objectives of their clients. They typically work with other professionals in various fields to provide their clients quality service to ensure that their needs are met.

Using this holistic approach, for example, an elder law attorney will address estate planning issues and will counsel clients about planning for incapacity with alternative decision-making documents. This attorney will also assist clients in planning for possible long-term care needs, including nursing home care. Locating the appropriate type of care, coordinating private and public resources to finance the cost of care, and working to ensure the client's right to quality care are all part of the elder and special needs law practice.

Many lawyers who specialize in this practice are members of NAELA, the National Academy of Elder Law Attorneys. NAELA members are committed to continuing their legal education and enhancing the quality of services they provide their clients. So seeking out a NAELA member will ensure that you are getting the best possible advice.

Members are guided in their practice by NAELA's Aspirational Standards. The guidelines set forth by these standards address the professionalism and ethical behavior of NAELA member attorneys and are the product of much study and deliberation. NAELA past president Stuart D. Zimring says this about the NAELA Aspirational Standards: "The clients served by elder and special needs law attorneys are among society's most vulnerable, often coming to us at times in their lives when they are most in need of wise counsel and advice. Because of this unfortunate reality, many of us believe that we, as elder and special needs law attorneys, should aspire to a higher level of professional practice standards than other attorneys."

The Aspirational Standards build upon and supplement each state's professional responsibility rules, which mandate minimum requirements of conduct for attorneys to maintain their licenses.

Most individuals can benefit from having some of the legal documents in this book, such as a Power of Attorney or Will, and certainly many adults far younger than 55 need or already have these documents. What elder law attorneys bring to the table is the knowledge of how to plan for possible calamities that become more likely as one grows older. A young person who gets sick is likely to recover, while an elderly person may be more likely to need long-term care. Knowing how to help their clients prepare for such possibilities is what sets elder law attorneys apart from other lawyers.

Elder law attorneys regularly counsel people who have to face the types of questions you're facing. They understand what you're going through because, truth be told, they've heard it before. Rather than sit alone in front of a computer trying to figure out what's the best course of action, when you consult with an elder law attorney you'll get expert guidance. If you want, you can sit back and just allow the attorney to handle pretty much everything. All you'll have to do is answer the questions the lawyer will pose, which he or she will customize to your particular situation, and then sign the documents that the lawyer has created just for you. A good elder law attorney will make the process as painless as possible, offering all the hand-holding you might want at every step, assuring that you'll get the legal documents that will be the most productive for your particular situation. Again, each situation is different, and the many variables require a lot of fine-tuning to create documents that will best serve you and your family. This is not a process that benefits from cookie-cutter computer programs.

If you buy a computer program, you're faced with a complicated process that is going to take several hours to complete by yourself. It will be easy to procrastinate, as there's no deadline like April 15th forcing you to complete this task. Rather than take what you might consider a daunting and risky self-help approach, why not take a step-by-step approach instead? The first is simply to make a phone call to the offices of an elder law attorney to schedule an appointment. Making an appointment to see an attorney takes only one phone call. After that, the rest will fall into place.

So look at 55 as the "April 15th" of this aspect of your life. Don't allow yourself to go past this deadline or else it will just be harder and harder to meet as the years go by, even as it becomes more and more important.

Most elder law attorneys are also estate planning attorneys, and these types of law overlap in many areas. Elder law attorneys are knowledgeable about long-term care strategies, including entitlements like Medicare and Medicaid, and how to address the planning concerns of persons with disabilities or "special needs."

PRIVACY

A lawyer provides privacy. Very often an entire family will sit down with the lawyer—mother, father, and adult children—and the children may expect to have a say concerning the matters of a parent. But after an initial meeting, the lawyer will often ask the other family members to leave and will make the final decisions, in complete privacy, with those persons represented and signing the papers. Not every family needs that privacy, and that's fine. But sometimes it's important. Let's say you don't like your daughter-in-law. Then perhaps you may wish to leave your son's share to his children so she'll never inherit anything directly. Could you discuss that in front of your son? Of course not, as his feelings would likely be hurt. But in a lawyer's office, when it's just you and the lawyer, you can freely discuss every option and choose the one that you feel is right for you.

Here's an example of a situation that lawyers encounter and why they understand how important it is that conversations with clients are and remain private, even from the client's children:

There was a family in which a husband and wife wanted to prepare a Will and Trust. They had three children, all with children of their own. One son was recently divorced and remarried. He was anxious to have his parents complete their estate plan because he had gone through such a rough time with his own divorce and legal entanglements. He accompanied his parents to the lawyer's office and had a great deal to say about what his parents should do. His opinions were very strong. The son's relationships with his ex-wife and his own children were strained from the divorce and his very quick remarriage. The son's children were very angry with their father and were refusing to see him.

The grandparents were caught in the middle of this emotional turmoil, but their relationship with their own children and with their son's estranged children was still warm and important to them. The parents' feelings on how to deal with the grandchildren were mixed. The lawyer wisely asked to see the parents alone, without the son, because his opinions added to their confusion. Once they were alone with the attorney they could express their disappointment in their son's rush to remarry and their deep sadness about the broken relationship with his children. They were almost tempted to give his inheritance to his children directly and skip him. They feared he was being foolish and would just squander the money on his new wife.

In the privacy of her office, the lawyer was able to help them sort through their mixed feelings and come up with a solution to the son's share between the son and his children. The parents then safeguarded the children's share in a Trust to be managed for them until they reached a mature age. The Trust would not be managed by either the remarried son or his ex-wife, but by their other children. The parents were relieved to find a solution that they could not have comfortably discussed in their son's presence. When the son was invited back in the room, with the parents' permission, the attorney outlined the estate plan as a done deal that was not open for discussion. This took away the awkwardness for the parents, who had found it difficult to explain their concerns to their son.

Another situation that may arise has to do with older parents who don't speak English very well and bring a family member, often a son or daughter, to translate for them. If the parents are leaving everything equally to their children, that might be fine, but what if that is not their intention? Perhaps they intend to leave their estate to all their children equally on entering the lawyer's office, but on hearing what the lawyer has to say, realize that they want to divide their estate in unequal shares. In some situations like this, it is better to have a disinterested party who is not in the Will—a friend or another professional, such as an accountant—act as translator.

One concern that people may have about seeing a lawyer is that the lawyer will try to convince them that, in addition to the five documents, they need more legal work. There's a good chance she will, but doesn't your doctor tell you to lose weight and possibly get another treatment, such as a colonoscopy, when you are in the examination room for a different issue? It doesn't mean that you have to do it; it only means that in a perfect world, you'd follow that advice. The same thing holds true when it comes to legal matters. In an ideal world, you'd want to be protected against every possible legal danger, but you don't live in an ideal world and you're free to say no. On the other hand, you may have some particular need that you aren't aware of and signing up for some additional legal work may make perfect sense.

Some people don't like to go to lawyers because they don't want to reveal too much about themselves. But holding back information can be counterproductive and even harmful. If you don't tell your

Keep in mind that what you tell a lawyer remains confidential.

doctor that you get short of breath when you go up a set of stairs, your doctor may not be able to help you prevent an impending heart attack. The same holds true for lawyers. Lawyers ask personal questions not because they are nosy, but because they want to prepare documents that will cover your particular needs. Keep in mind that what you tell a lawyer remains confidential. Unless you reveal that you're about to kill or harm someone (and the lawyer believes you have the means to do so), lawyers are legally bound not to pass on what they hear in their law office, so your secrets are safe. Client confidentiality is a cornerstone of legal practice.

The following is an example of how all five documents can come into play:

A father who was recently diagnosed with cancer had five sons. He lived in a brownstone in an up-and-coming neighborhood in which he and his wife had brought up the children. Two sons had helped him renovate the house, and the entire family was proud of the historic nature of the house and the neighborhood. One son, single (middle birth order), lived in the house with the father after having moved back in to assist his father after his mother died. The other four sons, all married, some with children, are all involved in their father's life and are close to one another. Two sons are within a fifty mile radius of Dad's home and two live at a distance. After his diagnosis of cancer, Dad received a prognosis that he had about two years to live if the prescribed treatments did not succeed.

Prior to this illness, Dad was able to handle everything. He missed his wife and liked having his son with him. In fact, his son who lived with him often joked that Dad was really taking care of him. After his illness progressed, the chemotherapy treatments to fight the cancer made Dad a bit weak and he started to need more help. The brothers rallied and the two who lived closer came on the weekends to help out. All was going well, but Dad was getting weaker and weaker, so they knew they needed to take some legal steps. Dad's Will dated back to when Mom was alive and the sons were teenagers. Their deceased mother and her very old brother, their uncle, were named the executors and nothing else was in place.

All five sons and their father made an appointment with an elder law attorney. Dad insisted that all five sons take part in this meeting, even though it would mean that he was giving up his right to make decisions in private. Dad felt that given his current fragile state, it was better to have all five sons participate as they might be better able to understand the ramifications of what the lawyer was presenting. The two long-distance sons attended by phone and the others came in person. It was a hectic meeting, with all parties trying to get their ideas across and be heard. It took awhile to sort out the issues and identify what the father wanted.

The first issues to be decided concerned Dad's health and care. He wanted to stay at home where he would be the most comfortable, and he wanted to continue being treated for cancer as long as there was a possible benefit. He had a strong will, and wanted to live and have as much control as possible. To accomplish this, he was presented with the idea of signing several legal documents setting forth his choices concerning his illness, care, finances, and other wishes should he be unable to handle his affairs. The documents suggested by the lawyer were the Health Care Proxy, the Living Will, and the Power of Attorney. All these documents sounded familiar to the dad and his sons, but they really needed the lawyer to explain each one so they could be sure they would use them effectively.

The process began with the Health Care Proxy and the Living Will, since Dad's current cancer condition was on the top of his worry list. The Health Care Proxy would allow him to appoint one of his sons to make medical decisions for him when he was unable to make them himself. So he chose his "live-in" son first and his oldest son who lived in the neighboring state as his second choice. His reasoning was the "live-in" son was right there with him and already knew about his illnesses and medications. The oldest son was also nearby, and all the brothers respected him. Dad also said, "My oldest son also has the best 'mouthpiece.' He can talk to anyone and they become his friends, so he'll get the doctors to do right by me." This was sound reasoning, and as a result he received excellent care.

In dealing with signing a Living Will, Dad was more hesitant. He wanted to receive treatment and was not ready to make an advance decision to terminate medical treatment. Dad felt that by signing a Living Will he would be "giving up." When he realized that his son as his agent could control how the Living Will would be used, he considered it. The son, as health care agent, could keep this document private and not put it into his medical records until it was determined Dad would no longer benefit from treatment. He laughingly then agreed and told his son, "Okay, hold on to it until I am about 95 years old and then you can tell them I don't want any machines to keep me alive, because that is how old I plan to live to." After the jokes, which helped to release a bit of fear, Dad agreed that if he was in a terminal condition with no hope of recovery, then the Living Will could be useful.

The next part of the discussion turned to the need for a Power of Attorney (POA) to appoint an agent for legal and financial *affairs. Dad understood the need for this right away. He said, "This is about my house and my money. Who will be in charge?" He already had gone over all the bills with his live-in son, as he admitted that he sometimes experienced "chemo brain." Once he sent his son to the bank to get some money for him and it was a big "to-do" with phone calls and letters back and forth with the bank. The previous week he had his son made joint owner on his checking account for convenience. The other brothers were surprised to learn this and asked how much was in the checking account. Dad told them there was about $30,000. This caused a bit of a ripple when Dad and the family learned that the money in the joint account would become the legal property of the live-in son on Dad's death. That wasn't Dad's intent, although he said that maybe it was okay since his son could use the money to bury him if it was needed. He emphasized that everything was to be divided evenly among the five sons and none given to others, even to the grandchildren.*

Dad selected the same two sons to be named as agents under the POA and named the other sons as alternates. Thus, all five sons were named to serve as possible agents in a pecking order, two as primary agent, and three in backup positions as alternate agents. He gave them full powers to act on his behalf in any legal or financial matters.

The next issue to be addressed was Dad's need to update his Will. His brownstone, as a result of his sweat equity and loving restoration, along with a change in the neighborhood, was valued at over one million dollars. He wanted all five sons to share in that inheritance but did not want his "live-in" son to find himself without a home after he had "sacrificed" his own home to move in with his father. He agreed that his Will would give this son the right to reside in the property for five years after his death and to collect the rent from the second apartment to use to maintain the house. After five years the son would agree to either buy out his brothers' shares at the then market value or sell the building and move out so the sales proceeds could be equally divided. This plan was described in the new Will so all knew what to expect. This settled any disagreements as the father set the tone that this was his wish. Dad also made it clear that the estate would be shared among the sons only and not the grandchildren. This was unusual, but he explained how he had been helping all along with the grandchildren's education and now he wanted to focus on his sons only.

Finally Dad, an avid computer user, had all kinds of online accounts, including a whole collection of photos stored in the cloud. He believed in storing everything on his computer, and had files and disks and thumb drives for everything. Some things were encrypted, while others were protected by passwords. What he didn't have was an easy directory for his sons to gain access to his computer files and data. The lawyer implored him to create a digital diary so that his digital assets could be saved and accessed, as needed, or discontinued.

Dad also needed to provide authorization to his appointed agents so they could get into his online accounts, computer valuables, and other stored information. The lawyer and the sons helped Dad organize this information and researched what authorizations needed to be in place to allow access both in life and after death.

As a result of this comprehensive approach, Dad was ready to face his illness and his sons were equipped with the right tools to assist him. There would be bumps in the road, as serious illness such as cancer is never easy to deal with, but at least this family had a clear legal road map to follow. The father had given his sons the gifts of clarity and peace by sharing his wishes with them and providing them with the means to get there.

~

Document 1: The Health Care Proxy

*A Health Care Proxy is a document in which
you appoint an agent to make health care decisions
for you if you are unable to do so.*

So what happens to you if you're in a hospital and unable to communicate for whatever reason? Who calls the shots for you and your care? Obviously not you, since you can't even call out for pizza. You may think it's your doctor, but that begs the question: Who precisely is your doctor? In the current hospital scene, your treating physician may be one of many health care professionals handling your care. If something happened to you while you were out of town, your doctor would be whoever happened to be on call at the hospital. If you want to put someone whom you trust in charge of your health care decision making, your best option is to sign a Health Care Proxy (HCP), or Health Care Directive. This document appoints a specific person—your health care agent—to make decisions for you and to discuss these decisions and other aspects of your health condition with your doctor, when and if you are unable to do so. (In some states an HCP is called a Health Care Power of Attorney, Medical Directive, or Health Care Surrogate.)

Before proceeding any further, it is important to point out that you, through this appointed surrogate, can have some say in decision making, even if you are in a deep coma. The first thing everyone thinks when they hear about a health care agent's power is the idea of "pulling the plug"; that is, the agent decides that because there is minimal to zero chance of your brain functioning again you should be disconnected from any machines and/or medications and allowed to die. But the real value of having a health care agent in place is that he or she can make *routine* medical decisions that you cannot make for yourself, as well as end-of-life choices. The following is an example:

> *Judie had a client whose mother had become very ill in a local hospital and died. As a result, the entire family, including my client, had a fear of this particular hospital. When she needed an immediate admission for surgery, her daughter, the health care agent, was able to arrange an admission to a different hospital, which greatly enhanced her mother's confidence in the treatment she was getting and actually helped her overall recovery. Once empowered, the daughter/agent was able to oversee her mother's physical therapy and intervene about her hospital diet to be sure she was given the right food, as well as attend to other small details that made her mother much more comfortable. It was also vital to have the daughter present when the team of doctors breezed into the mother's hospital room to give her a jargon-filled description of her illness. Luckily, the daughter had the authority to be on hand to listen and figure out what was being said. She had the right to ask questions and make suggestions as well. Her mother was far from incapacitated, but she was pretty foggy from the surgery and not in the best shape to ask questions and be a real advocate for herself. The presence and help of her health care agent, who could freely discuss her mother's medical options and view her mother's medical records, was invaluable.*

When you are incapacitated, having an HCP in place ensures that *your* wishes (not your agent's wishes) are honored. (For an example of this, see the draft of an HCP in Appendix B: Heath Care Proxy.) To whatever extent you wish, you can ask your attorney to include detailed instructions in your HCP regarding your care and treatment in specific situations. If your HCP says that everything must be done to keep you alive, then that's what has to happen. (In some states a Living Will, which is described in detail in Chapter Three, may be used to direct decision-making at the end of life.)

State laws vary when it comes to most legal documents and that's true of the HCP. So the exact wording and name for an HCP may differ from state to state, but in general the principles behind the HCP are the same in all states.

An HCP is what is referred to as an "Advance Directive," meaning that you have put down on paper ahead of time your wishes concerning your health care treatment and whom you want to handle medical matters. The goal of the HCP is to appoint an agent to act on your behalf if a physician determines that you are unable to make medical decisions for yourself. This doesn't necessarily mean that you have to be in a coma for the HCP to take effect. For example, perhaps you are in so much pain that the doctors have decided it is best to keep you heavily sedated. (This frequently happens if you need to be intubated, as most people would pull the tubes going down their throat out if they were fully conscious.) Or perhaps you develop dementia that prevents you from making your own health care decisions.

Let's assume for a moment that you don't have an HCP. Do you remember the Terri Schiavo case? This involved the Florida woman who was entirely incapacitated for many years but in stable condition and not at any risk of dying. Terri's husband and parents were at odds about whether or not to keep her on life support. It made news all over the country, and the case went all the way to the Supreme Court. While you might think that without an HCP it would still be evident who would make the decisions for you and that your case would not be like the Schiavo case, according to the courts, it's not so evident at all. Family members and loved ones can have differing but deeply felt opinions about end-of-life decisions, which can create turmoil that can last months and even years.

Beyond "pulling the plug," there could be many other decisions that need to be made if you are unable to do so. The person named as your agent in the HCP would be the one to make those nonlife-determining decisions, which could include whether you should you join a drug trial, be placed in a rehabilitation center, be discharged to hospice, and so on. Moreover, to make decisions in your best interest, your agent should have the same access to your medical records that you would have. The agent would be entitled to ask for a second opinion or have you moved to another facility, perhaps one with better equipment and a more experienced staff, or to the care of another doctor, such as a specialist. Having these sorts of decisions made on your behalf while you're unable to do so could save your life, or improve the quality of your life once you leave the hospital.

When preparing your HCP, you may want to consult with your family physician as well as your lawyer. If your health care proxy includes instructions that are too broadly stated, your wishes may be misunderstood. If you don't know much about science or medicine, you might not be prepared to state your wishes in every circumstance. And you certainly would want to get treatment in the event of an illness from which you could probably recover. Some broad guidelines, with the proper wording, cover most situations you might face. And if you have certain expectations, say, certain diseases that you are more likely to be affected by because of your family history, your doctor may be able to give you some direction regarding what your HCP should state. In the event you were later to be diagnosed with another disease that could generate different medical needs, such as Alzheimer's, you might consider providing your agent with updated instructions at that time. The health care agent can adapt his or her approach to your changing health status. This flexibility is a major benefit of naming a caring individual to act as your representative.

Speaking of physicians, a majority have this paperwork in place for themselves. This is because they've seen the pain and suffering of disease and accidents up close, so they want to exert as much control over such situations as they can. For example, many doctors decide not to undergo some of the more onerous cancer treatments if they know that all the treatments will do is prolong their life briefly while adding greatly to their suffering. Patients may prefer to spend their last days on earth fully capable of enjoying time with their family rather than be incapacitated because of the serious side effects that such treatments carry. But, of course, that is a very personal decision. To maintain control over such decisions, having completed the proper paperwork is vital.

Don't assume that others would make the same decision for you that they would make for themselves:

> *There was the case of an older gentleman who was dying from a long, painful terminal illness and had no Health Care Proxy. He was no longer able to communicate or eat, and his doctor suggested that, to avoid the final pain and suffering he was likely to endure during his last days, nothing further be done with regard to feeding him. However, the man's only child insisted that a feeding peg be inserted into his stomach so that he could be fed. Since the doctor didn't want to be sued afterward for starving the patient to death, he performed the procedure, even though he knew that this was only going to prolong the man's suffering. The patient died three weeks after a feeding peg was inserted. The son, who loved his father very much, was understandably very emotional, and though he meant well, his inability to accept his father's terminal condition may have caused more harm than good. It certainly caused the doctor to take actions that he felt were not in the patient's best interests.*

YOUR HEALTH CARE AGENT'S RESPONSIBILITIES

Being a health care agent is a serious responsibility. Therefore, to ensure that your agent properly handles his or her duties as the need arises, you should have an in-depth conversation with this person so that he or she really understands your wishes in the various situations that might arise. Sometimes people agree to be your agent in a pro forma manner, saying, "Oh, sure you can put me on your HCP because you're healthy as a horse and nothing's going to happen to you." Judie recounts the following example of how such an attitude can backfire:

Early in my career when I had very few clients, a "neighbor" who was single asked me to be her health care agent. She was a vibrant 60-year-old woman who worked in the local hospital running their gift shop. She owned her own apartment, had savings, and had just purchased long-term-care insurance. I thought this would be an easy one and that I could handle it. Now, she is 86 years old and has serious dementia. I am in charge of her total care, including hiring home care workers, setting up her doctor appointments, and keeping her safe at home. So my "Oh, sure, I can do it for you" has become a full-time responsibility. I now encourage my clients to fully discuss the possibility of their needing care with their appointed agent. It helps to know what someone wants and needs in order to be comfortable. Fortunately, I had twenty years to get to know my client and that has made it possible for me to help her in ways that work for her. Take the time to talk to your agent. Prepare him or her to care for you appropriately and in the manner that you wish.

As you can see, it's all well and good to agree to be a health care agent when looking at the person's current health, but anyone, no matter how healthy, can have a serious accident at any moment. So in addition to having an HCP appointing an agent, you need to let this person know how you feel about your health care, including your feelings about treatment as your health changes over time. You should also update your agent as the years go by, as needed, if your views or health condition changes. (You will also be appointing an alternate agent, so you need to have the same conversations with the alternate.)

Your agent also has to know who your doctors are (including your general practitioner and any specialists) and how to contact them. It is a good idea to give your doctors a copy of your HCP so that if there is ever the need for your agent to contact one of your doctors, the HCP will be in your medical records. Anything you can do to increase the odds of your agent getting full cooperation from medical providers is a wise move. This is especially true if there is a medical emergency and time is of the essence. You also need to provide your agent with a list of all your medications. Such a list is the first thing a doctor or hospital asks for. If an emergency room doctor needed this information and you were unable to provide it, your agent should be prepared to do so. (And as your medications change, don't forget to let your agent know. Keep a dated running list of medications available with your important paperwork to post and save. Ask your pharmacist for a printed list.)

Joanne was the health care agent for her 94-year-old great-aunt Mary, who had multiple health problems. Mary was being moved to an assisted-care facility, which required that a full set of prescriptions be given to its nursing staff. But during this process, Mary encountered some health problems that caused changes to her prescriptions, including some made by her personal physicians and some made by physicians in the hospital. Keeping track of all these changes was a complicated task, seemingly too complicated even for the physicians, who failed to notify Joanne of the critical changes in Mary's medications. Luckily, Joanne found the new prescriptions, checked them against the old medication list, and was able to instruct the home care nurse to give Mary the proper new medications. Had Joanne not been attentive, her aunt would have suffered serious and possibly fatal consequences. Mary, in part because of poor eyesight, was unable to handle this duty, yet, as it turned out, her life depended on someone watching over what was happening.

Without having been appointed agent in a written HCP while her aunt was able to make the decision to do so, Joanne would have been unable to examine Mary's medical records, communicate with her doctors and other health care professionals, and make decisions for her beloved aunt when she could no longer focus on medical issues or make decisions.

This story illustrates the importance of choosing the right person to be your agent. This person must have the time and personal devotion to watch out for your best interests. It's not easy, but having no one fully in charge can actually be life threatening.

DEMENTIA AND OTHER CONSIDERATIONS

Dementia is a growing problem in our society. While it may take longer for the victim of dementia to lose the ability to make medical decisions, it's almost inevitable that the day will come. Therefore, appointing a health care agent in an HCP is vital at the first diagnosis of dementia or any other cognitive impairment. It is also important to inform an agent you may have already designated of your condition. A person who was willing to be your agent in an emergency may not be so willing to continue as your agent if he or she knows that the duties may become weekly, if not daily, and may last for quite some time.

There are a few other things to consider when choosing your agent. One factor is how much the person you are considering is attuned to your medical condition and your wishes. The more interested in health matters your agent is, the better he or she will be able to grasp what your doctors will have to say. In fact, if you have any relatives who are in the medical profession, you might consider asking one of them to be your agent. Some people get queasy when it comes to discussing medical issues and would prefer not to know the details. That type of person shouldn't be your health care agent because speaking with your medical team is an integral part of the job. Your agent be both smart and forceful enough to ask questions and insist that the doctor or medical facility obey orders given by the agent. Of course, if other family members expect to be involved in some capacity, this person needs to have sufficient diplomatic skills to be able to consult with them while still keeping your wishes and best interests in the forefront. (Again, remember the Terri Schiavo case, where family members went to war via the courts.)

Your agent should also have the time required to be of assistance. Doctors in hospitals rarely make exact appointments. When they say they'll be by your bedside in the morning, that could mean 6 A.M., 9

A.M., or 3 P.M. If decisions have to be made, your agent may have to be there at any time. So even though your son, for example, is the one in your family who would best understand what the doctor was saying, if he runs his own business and has a hectic schedule, he may not be available at the hospital for important consultations. That may also mean that your agent needs to live nearby, though not necessarily, if he or she has the ability and time to travel to you.

In other words, you need to do some careful thinking about whom to appoint. (However, don't let that stop you from having an HCP!) You also may have to change your agent from time to time. For example, you might have appointed your sister as your agent, but if she moves out of town, then consider changing the form and making her an alternate. Of course, you hope you never need an HCP, but once you've decided to prepare one, only you can select your agent; it is not a decision that a lawyer can make for you. The lawyer will ask you questions and guide you to some extent, but the lawyer doesn't know every one of your available friends and family members and certainly won't know who gets along with whom and who doesn't. There have been some situations in which a child who has lived far away for a long time arrives on the scene in a health care emergency and tries to wrest control of the parent's medical care, much to the disturbance of the patient and other family members. Illness can bring out the worst, as well as the best, in families.

> **Your agent should be forceful enough to insist that doctors obey orders given by the agent.**

CHOOSING AN OUTSIDER

A nurse friend of ours told us the story of an elderly Hispanic mother with a large family. She became ill, in fact she was dying, and the best course would have been to let her die at home peacefully under hospice care, with nurses visiting regularly to make sure she wasn't in pain. She didn't have an HCP, but even if she had appointed a family member as her agent, the fights that broke out over her care among family members would probably not have ended the family's turmoil. Half the family members agreed that she should be left to die peacefully while the other half insisted that everything be done to keep her alive.

Family members will sometimes make an agent who decides to withhold treatment to a dying person feel guilty. Moreover, in the previous case, had nothing been done the resulting split might have caused permanent separation among family members. In this case, the mother had to undergo five separate hospital visits, with all the invasive procedures and discomfort those entailed, and she still died shortly thereafter. Did those visits prolong her life? Possibly for a month or so, but given all that she had to go through, the far better course would have been to let her die at home when the time had arrived.

So if you believe that your family may be similar to the one discussed here, the better choice for your HCP agent could be someone outside the family. That person would be far less emotional and would consider only your best interests when it came time to make decisions. And even if some members of your family later wanted nothing to do with this agent, at least the family would remain intact.

HOW TO CHOOSE YOUR HEALTH CARE AGENT

Don't make the assumption that the person closest to you, such as your eldest child, should automatically be your health care agent. Instead, make a list and write down next to each name the pros and cons of each potential candidate. There are a number of important characteristics your agent should have. You should consider his or her availability, personality, and level of understanding of medical language. You may not have anyone on your list who scores a perfect ten in all categories. For example, your daughter who lives next door would score highest when it comes to proximity, but if she is a single mother with three young children for whom you babysit when she goes to work, it might be impossible for her to be at your bedside if you wind up in the hospital.

So this is a decision that you can't allow only your heart to decide. It requires a lot of thought. And if you decide to choose someone besides the obvious candidate, such as the daughter who lives next door, make sure to explain to her why you are not choosing her so that she understands and her feelings aren't hurt. If you can find an agent who promises to consult with her, that will make her feel better about your decision. And you can make her the alternate HCP agent so that she could step in if she's available but won't feel pressured into it.

If there are no family members whom you want to appoint as your health care agent, you can appoint a close family friend or even a family physician. There are even cases where people have close family but *prefer* someone outside the family to make health care decisions. This may be due to the lack of confidence in the family members or just the nature of the relationship with the non-family member. Domestic partners are a good example of non-family members who are typically appointed as HCP agents.

You can take your list of potential candidates to your attorney and get his or her opinion, but the final decision will be yours. Hopefully, you'll never need the services of this HCP agent, but if you choose the best candidate, you can tell yourself that you're in the best possible hands should something happen to you.

WHEN THERE IS NO HCP

If you do not have an HCP and are incapacitated, often someone can still act as a surrogate. The doctors by default may ask a close relative or friend who had been regularly visiting to be the surrogate if the state law allows surrogates to step in. Some states have laws that direct who will serve as your automatic agent, if you fail to appoint one, under the theory that this person will substitute his or her judgment for you and act in your best interest. This may work in an emergency, but obviously it's better for you to decide ahead of time whom you want to serve in this capacity. Some states authorize doctors to decide. They then consult with a relative whom they feel may be able to handle health care decisions. Alternatively, as a last resort when there are no legal alternatives, a court may be requested to appoint a guardian to make these decisions. The court-appointed guardian might not even be someone you know, but rather someone the judge knows who will be given a fee for acting as a guardian. Certainly that's not a situation you want to be in while you're incapacitated.

Each state has different laws regarding what happens when there is no Health Care Proxy. One common statute says that in such cases the immediate family, such as the children, get to decide. But what if the children disagree? Let's say Mom has Alzheimer's disease and needs to move to a nursing home or an assisted-living facility. Because she has no Health Care Proxy, the state allows her two daughters to decide. But the two sisters have strong and very different opinions. The court will now decide to see which sister is appointed guardian, a frequently long and costly process. In the meantime, Mom remains at home and in danger due to her limited mental capacity while the fight continues between her daughters.

You might assume that your children will always get along and be levelheaded, and so you trust them to be able to make such decisions together. But when you add stress to a situation—and making important health care decisions is always stressful because it means someone you love is very sick—the dynamics of even the best relationship can change. Putting one person in charge isn't necessarily the perfect solution. Arguments can still break out if you appoint an agent, but at least those arguments are less likely to be decided in a costly and time-consuming court proceeding because, in the end, a single person is in charge and will make the final decision.

There is one more point to make. An elder law attorney will ask you questions to help you decide which person to put in charge. Afterward, you can say to your children, "After consulting with my lawyer, I decided to appoint Cathy." Being able to say that your decision was based on the advice of your attorney may make it easier for everyone to ultimately accept this decision, particularly if there is some push-back from family members who were not chosen.

AVOIDING SURPRISES

Another reason to have an HCP is to avoid the type of surprise that occurred in the following case:

> *Susan, an elderly woman with advanced dementia, told the visiting nurse that her nephew, Lou, who lived out of state, was in charge of her affairs. When Susan took a turn for the worse, the nurse contacted Lou, who said that this was the first he'd heard of the arrangement and that to his knowledge no actual paperwork had been done. Lou loved his aunt and was willing to help in any way he could, but he had no official standing.*
>
> *One day when the visiting nurse arrived at the apartment, she found that a strange man had moved in with Susan. It turned out he was a different nephew, Sal, who lived in Canada. The problem was, when Sal's mother had died of cancer, Sal got the idea into his head that it was the pain medication that had killed her, not her disease. And so Sal did everything in his power to prevent the nurse from giving any pain medication to his aunt during the last month of her life, leading to a great deal of unnecessary pain and suffering.*
>
> *The whole team at the visiting nurse service held meetings about this case in the hope of convincing Sal to assist with the administration of pain medication. His denial of pain management and comfort care went against everything they stood for, which was the prevention of suffering. But since there was no paperwork, even Lou, when he came to town for a visit, couldn't do anything about it as Sal was more than adamant about "protecting" his aunt. Of course Susan died, spending the last month in excruciating pain.*

Susan had believed that she'd signed some papers, though in fact she had not. This case illustrates not only why you should have the proper paperwork prepared, but why you should do so in a timely fashion, no later than age 55. You may believe that if something were to happen to your health, then matters would go according to some plan you had in place. But without the proper legal underpinning, your plan may fall prey to unexpected surprises.

CHAPTER THREE

Document 2: The Living Will and End-of-Life Choices

A Living Will allows you to leave instructions about the care you want to receive at the end of your life if you are unable to give those instructions.

A Living Will, or End-of-Life Directive, is a document in which you specify what medical treatment you would like to receive if you are near death with little or no hope of recovery and are unable to give those instructions yourself. In some states, the Living Will, which is a personal statement from you, can be enhanced by a doctor's order. This doctor's order can be a Medical Directive to Doctors or Medical Order for Life-Sustaining Treatment (MOLST) or Physician Orders for Life-Sustaining Treatment (POLST). Some states do not have a specific legal form of the Living Will, but generally as long as whatever is in writing was signed before witnesses, it is enforceable. In some states, the Health Care Proxy (described in Chapter Two) has specific powers regarding end-of-life directions that can substitute for the Living Will.

Obviously no document dealing with end-of-life choices that is prepared ahead of time could state your intentions and philosophy about every type of medical emergency that might arise. Practically speaking, a Living Will is used to state your general wishes regarding what treatment you wish to receive, or *not* receive, when you are terminally ill and death is imminent. The Living Will answers the question of whether your doctors and family should do everything possible to keep you alive, or, alternatively, if they should withhold some treatments and simply focus on making you as comfortable as possible until the end arrives.

Doctors can only guess at how long a terminally ill person has to live, so it is best to have in place a health care agent (as described in the previous chapter) who understands the nuances of your desires and is able to make day-to-day decisions about your care. This is preferable to following the static directions in a document. But if there is no appointed agent, then the Living Will will be the sole source of instructions concerning end-of-life decisions. If there are medical decisions that you are unable to make for yourself at the time of need that do not have to do with end-of-life matters, the Living Will is on hold and it is the agent appointed in the HCP who will make the decisions under your physician's guidance.

The guidance a Living Will provides may make it easier for your health care agent to make the very difficult decision about whether or not it is time to "pull the plug"—that is, to terminate life support measures or treatments that serve merely to prolong your dying. Often, these instructions also are part of the HCP. But the Living Will, since it is a more limited document, makes your desires much clearer. If you've signed a Living Will stating you don't want any extreme measures taken to extend your life—such as in the case, for example, that your doctor states you will never regain consciousness—then you've underlined that point.

Could you have a Living Will without an HCP? Yes, but remember, it's much more likely that the agent you specify in the HCP will be called in to make decisions in situations where it's not a matter of life and death. For example, if you've just had major surgery and are under heavy sedation and a decision needs to be made regarding future emergency surgery, your health care agent is going to do that. So while the Living Will takes care of a very important decision—under what circumstances you wish to be kept alive—in the vast majority of cases what you really need will be covered by the HCP.

The following case illustrates a worst-case scenario of what can happen when the proper papers have not been prepared:

Doris held her assets jointly with her daughter and her second husband, believing that joint ownership offered her sufficient legal protection and that she really didn't need to take any other legal actions to protect herself. When she was in her early 80s she fell gravely ill. Her doctors said that she would never recover and recommended that she be allowed to die. Doris had remarried and had no Advance Directives or legal documents stating her wishes for health care.

Her second husband, as the next of kin, legally speaking, held the first position as a medical surrogate with the legal right to decide her care choices, not her daughter. Although the daughter knew that Doris would not want to be kept alive in such a situation, the husband's decision was to have the doctors do everything possible to keep her alive, so he approved the insertion of a tube to help her breathe. Since the tube in her throat was very uncomfortable, she resisted and so had to have her arms tied down to keep her from pulling the tubes out.

Doris's husband was 88 at the time, and while not suffering from dementia, he wasn't thinking clearly but reacting emotionally. The rest of her family watched in horror as Doris suffered terribly, day after day, for several months until she finally passed away. Had Doris drafted a Living Will to make her end-of-life wishes clear, her daughter might have been able to insist that Doris be allowed to die more peacefully and not be kept alive with a breathing tube.

While it's impossible to predict the future, a lawyer with years of experience working with clients and their families in similar situations will be able to recommend the legal solutions that reflect your wishes, and offer you properly prepared documents so you can avoid the sort of trap that waylaid Doris.

~

Document 3: The Power of Attorney

A Power of Attorney is a legal document that gives
someone you choose the power to act in your place.

Television shows, movies, and even commercials often use a deceased's Will in the plot, so everyone is pretty much familiar with this kind of document. And while there's no doubt that having a Will is very important (and is a subject discussed in detail in Chapter Five), let's face it, a Will only comes into play after you're no longer in the picture. If at that point things don't work out exactly right, how concerned are you going to be?

But plenty of things, health-related or not, can happen to you while you're still alive and kicking that can render you temporarily incapacitated or unable to act on your own behalf. It is for such circumstances that a Power Of Attorney (POA) is needed. For example, you take a cruise, the ship's engine catches fire, and you're stuck in the middle of the ocean for a week. It's been known to happen. In the meantime, your son gets arrested and you want to arrange bail for him, but you're thousands of miles away stranded on a boat that's bobbing on the deep blue sea. Perhaps you were also due back to sign papers to refinance your mortgage, and your failure to sign by the deadline will result in having to pay a higher interest rate. The only thing that might save the day in such situations is to have the trusted agent you appointed in your Power of Attorney document act on your behalf.

A POA can allow your agent to step into your shoes and act for you in any number of ways. Your POA agent, for example, can sign your checks, renew your lease, or go to your bank and withdraw cash for you. As later discussed, the powers you give can be limited to certain actions or include virtually all actions.

Some people think lawyers are too pushy when it comes to the subject of the POA. But if you heard the horror stories that lawyers encounter—from the inability to access funds at a critical moment, to a house going into foreclosure, to cars being repossessed, to the failure to get medical care—all because the owner was unable to act, you'd be pushy, too. Here's one real example (witnessed by co-author Joanne):

Picture a wife on the stand in a courtroom. The judge is asking her personal questions, and as she answers, tears are streaming down her face. Her husband is in the hospital, very ill and unable to communicate, and she has two young children at home. Because most of their money is in accounts that are only in her husband's name, she now needs to undergo the difficult and intrusive legal process of being appointed guardian over her husband's property in order to access funds to pay their bills. All because her husband hadn't signed a POA yet—and he was a lawyer!

And here's another case:

Sally is a single, childless, 80-year-old former secretary (retired fifteen years) living in her own co-op in Brooklyn. Her only relatives are two nephews who live out of state, children of her deceased brother, Mike. They visit her several times a year and call her once every couple of months. Sally has few friends and shows signs of dementia. One day she rings her neighbor's bell, dazed and confused, possibly having suffered a stroke. The neighbor calls emergency medical services and Sally ends of up in the hospital for four weeks. Since the hospital can't locate any relatives and Sally can't live at home on her own, the hospital sends her to a nursing home.

Her nephews try contacting her, but she doesn't answer her phone and they have no way of finding her. Finally, after several months, they track her down at the nursing home. They immediately engage a lawyer to visit Aunt Sally at the nursing home to make a POA and Health Care Proxy so they can help their aunt. But when the lawyer goes to see Sally, she discovers that Sally is no longer able to understand the nature of her actions and therefore can't sign any documents. The lawyer also reports back to the nephews that an institutional guardian was just appointed by the court at the request of the nursing home, which is seeking payment of its monthly charges. This guardian, who doesn't know Sally and has never even met her, is now in charge of all her affairs and will also make health care decisions for her, without the input of her family members.

The nephews are devastated upon hearing this news. They can spend a lot of money going to court to try to overturn the guardianship, but more often than not, given that Sally never signed any papers and now isn't physically up to it, the courts won't grant such a request. So because Sally had done no legal planning, her co-op will be sold and its contents emptied and sold to pay for her nursing home expenses. There will be no opportunity to pass on her precious valuables, or any of her assets, to her loved ones. And her nephews are blocked from participating in her care decisions, including the selection of her place of residence for the rest of her life.

Bear in mind that these examples are not rarities but everyday occurrences. When someone becomes mentally or physically incapacitated and doesn't have the necessary paperwork in place, a bad situation is likely to get a lot worse.

THE POWER OF A POA

What can your agent do with a POA? That's up to you. You can give very broad powers, allowing him or her to do virtually anything you could do (except make a Will for you), or you could place limits on the agent's authority. Let's say you own a second home in another state. With a limited POA, you could give someone authority only to handle the sale of that property. Some, but not all, of the other common powers a POA can confer include making bank transactions, paying bills, handling all kinds of legal matters, gaining access to safe deposit boxes, dealing with retirement and insurance benefits, preparing and filing tax returns, exercising stockholder rights, applying for Medicare, Medicaid, or other government benefits, making gifts, changing the beneficiaries on your retirement accounts, re-titling bank accounts as joint accounts, and borrowing money. And a POA agent doesn't have to be limited to personal finances. If you own your own business, you can authorize your POA to assist you with your business; for example, to sign your name on payroll checks, if you are unable to do so yourself.

This happened to a client who owned a specialized jewelry business making fittings for such prestigious jewelry companies as Tiffany's. The business owner was a sole proprietor and the company was the main source of income for his wife and three children. One child had a disability and needed constant care. His wife was the child's primary caretaker and ran a small business from her home. The jewelry owner had a sudden heart attack and was unable to work for more than six months. His wife was frantic because she knew that all pending business orders were critically time sensitive. Besides knowing little about the workings of the business, she had no access to the business accounts or tax records.

Fortunately, her accountant and business lawyer were able to work with her elder law attorney to immediately have the husband execute a POA appointing his wife as his agent. Even though they lost two key jewelry orders as they could not make the deliveries on time, the delay was short-lived, as the wife was able to use the Power of Attorney as agent on behalf of her husband. If the husband had not retained his mental capacity, the months of delay it would have taken for the wife to be appointed as his guardian by the court in order to gain access and manage his business affairs could have resulted in a much more serious financial impact.

Most POAs become valid on the day they are signed and all POA signatures must be witnessed by a notary public. But you could execute a POA that wouldn't become valid until either a particular day or a point in time when you were incapable of acting for yourself. (This type of POA is called a "springing" POA, and is not legal in every state. More about these will follow.)

A LIMITED POA VERSUS A DURABLE POA

There are three basic types of POAs. Limited POAs are limited either by time or to particular acts or conditions upon which you authorize your agent to act. A limited POA may be in force as long as you are capable of handling your own affairs, in the legal sense. So let's say you had a serious leg injury and couldn't go to the bank but your mental facilities were fine. In that case, by a limited POA

Your failure to have a Durable POA may force those who care for you to go to court to be appointed your guardian.

you could appoint someone to do your banking for you. However, if you then had a stroke and were no longer mentally capable to direct your appointed representative, that limited POA would no longer be in effect. On the other hand, a General POA (GPOA) allows your agent to do virtually *anything* that you can do, but only as long as you are fully capable of handling these duties yourself.

A Durable POA (DPOA), however, is not only for the type of emergency described above, but also to handle situations where a long-term disability, like dementia, is growing progressively worse. The Durable POA is said to "survive throughout your incapacity," meaning that you've appointed someone who will be able to take care of your affairs until you die.

If you don't have a durable POA and you become mentally incapacitated, family members could go to court to have themselves appointed your guardian. But this is a time-consuming, emotion-draining, and costly court-involved proposition. And just because a person is appointed guardian doesn't mean that his or her court dealings are over. There will be a reporting procedure that will add to the burden. And it's not unheard of for more than one member of the family to petition for guardianship, leaving the courts to decide who will handle your affairs, usually after much fighting.

Of course not everybody has close family members. In that case, the court may be asked to intervene and will likely appoint a lawyer to act as guardian. This lawyer won't know your wishes and will be paid from your assets. So if you don't have close family members, it is even more important that you appoint a friend, colleague, or professional you trust as your POA agent. (The agent you name in the POA may be entitled to compensation, but it is often limited by law. Your attorney can offer good advice on this matter.)

MORE ABOUT POAS

A Durable POA can be written so that it doesn't become effective *until* you are incapacitated. This is called a "springing" POA because it does not "spring" into force until something happens to cause your incapacity or until you need another person to act for you. This may sound like a good idea, but there is a potential drawback. If your attorney-in-fact (also known as agent) goes to a bank and says, "So-and-so is incapacitated; here's a POA, and I need to take out some money," why should the bank believe this person? It is possible for your POA to describe what documents are needed to prove your incapacity, which may be certificates from one or more of your treating physicians attesting to your inability to make decisions for yourself. Unfortunately, in some cases, your agent may be forced to go to court to prove you are incapacitated when the necessity of going to court was exactly what you were trying to prevent in the first place.

However, if your POA agent encounters problems while you are still mentally capable, you could help smooth the way by letting the bank and any other relevant organizations know that you appointed this person as your agent. In general, springing POAs are less favorable and are not frequently used because of the difficulties in activating the powers, especially if medical professionals are required to determine incapacity.

Some banks will ask you to sign their own POA form that will cover only the accounts you have in their bank. Legally, they may not be able to require this special bank form and can be compelled to honor a valid POA approved by your state's law. Bank managers are cautious as they may have run into situations where money was withdrawn from their bank after a POA had been revoked but the bank was never notified. It should go without saying that if you ever decide to revoke a POA under which your agent was given banking powers, you should notify every bank and financial institution where you have accounts. But since not everyone does this, you can understand why a bank might have a policy that requires you to sign its own POA form. Since most bankers have witnessed situations where the bank has released money improperly, it makes sense that they would want to protect themselves, not to mention the accounts of their customers.

Can you force a bank to accept your perfectly legal POA? Sometimes having the lawyer who prepared the POA apply pressure on the bank is effective. Or else you could go to court, but that would take time and cost money, and the whole point of having a POA is to avoid just this type of situation. Your best bet is to check with your bank. If they absolutely insist that you sign their POA, that's probably the preferable option. Understanding that this situation might occur is what is important, so that you can prevent your agent from running into this particular roadblock at the exact moment in time when you need to have him or her act on your behalf.

As stated earlier, if you really want a springing POA, one way to make it more likely to be accepted is to include wording that says it becomes effective when one or more of your doctors, whom you name specifically, attests that you are incapacitated. In that way there would be someone in authority, your doctor, to help prove that you are incapacitated and that it was your wish to grant this POA.

If you ever change your mind about having someone continue to act as your POA agent, or if this person decides he or she no longer wants the responsibility, you can revoke or change your POA. Of course if your agent quits after you've become incapacitated, then appointing a new agent would be possible only if you gave the agent the power to delegate his or her power. It's always a good idea to name an alternate agent when drawing up your POA, or, to the extent allowed in your state, to give your POA agent the power to delegate any or all of the agent's power to a person the agent selects.

Durable POAs are recognized in all fifty states, provided they contain certain state-required language, such as the phrase "this Power of Attorney shall not be affected by subsequent disability or incapacity of the principal." In a few states, *all* POA forms are considered to be durable (even without special language stating so) as the underlying state law creates the durability. Generally, federal agencies such as the Social Security Administration do not recognize state-law created POAs. If the principal receives Social Security payments, a state-based POA is not accepted for the management of a beneficiary's benefits. The Social Security Administration recognizes only a "representative payee" instead of a Power of Attorney agent for handling beneficiary's funds. A representative's responsibilities include using benefits to pay for the current and foreseeable needs of the beneficiaries, saving any remaining benefits, and keeping good records of how the benefits are spent. A booklet that describes the process of being appointed a Social Security representative payee is available by calling 1-800-772-1213. You can also download the booklet at **www.socialsecurity. gov/pubs/10076.html**. You may also need to sign a separate POA for dealings with the Veterans Benefits Administration (the VA agent is called a fiduciary). You can access VA agency forms by logging onto **www.va.gov**. The IRS also has a special required form of POA, which can be located here: **www.irs.gov/pub/irs-pdf/f2848.pdf**. Check with your attorney concerning these specialized POAs.

> **Just because a person can't remember certain things doesn't mean he or she does not have the legal capacity to sign a POA or Will.**

One power *never* granted by a POA is the power to make a Will. That can only be done by you, and you have to be of sound mind to do so. Some people who have dementia wait too long and can no longer make a Will. However, bear in mind that dementia can take a long time to render a person unable to sign legal documents. Just because a person can't remember certain things doesn't mean he or she does not have the legal capacity to sign a POA or Will. An attorney asked to create such documents will always make sure that the person's mind is sufficiently sound to sign legal documents. The attorney can later certify to the validity of the POA or Will maker's mental capacity if anyone brings a challenge.

A SHORT-TERM POA

Sometimes you know ahead of time that you will be incapacitated or unavailable—for example, if you're going in for major surgery or away on an extended trip. In such instances you may want to have a POA that lasts only a limited amount of time. However, since accidents can always happen, and the main purpose of a POA is to help your family cope if something does happen to incapacitate you, it is usually preferable that the POA last indefinitely.

POAs VERSUS JOINT OWNERSHIP

Putting all or some of your assets in joint ownership with a family member or trusted person is one way of lessening the need for a POA, but this maneuver is not without its own set of risks. Here's another example that demonstrates what can happen with this strategy:

Let's say a mother makes her son a joint owner of her bank accounts. This son drives a truck for a living. One day he gets into a serious accident and is sued for more than his insurance covers. He loses the lawsuit and now the injured party goes after his assets to make up the difference in the court's verdict and the amount his insurance policy will pay. Since a portion of his assets consists of his mother's bank accounts, her savings could go toward paying for his lawsuit. In other words, the mother's funds that are held jointly with her son are fully available for attachment by any of her son's possible creditors.

For couples in which one spouse has a job where he or she is more likely to be sued, it is often suggested to put the majority of the assets in the sole name of the spouse who is less prone to being sued. So a doctor who is afraid of being sued for malpractice might put all his assets in his wife's name. But if something were to happen to the wife and she couldn't act independently or handle banking activities, these family assets would be unavailable. If the wife needed expensive health care and the husband didn't have POA authority, he wouldn't be able to access the assets he transferred to her to pay for her care or to cover the family's expenses.

In addition, even if all the assets you own are held jointly, you may not be able to access all of them. Stocks you own jointly require both signatures in order to be sold. If both your names are on the deed of your home, you both have to sign in order to sell your house. Without a POA, your spouse would not be able to name or change a beneficiary on your life insurance or retirement benefits. So each spouse having a POA for the other may be critically important if something were to happen to one of you. Joint ownership of assets does not cover you in these circumstances. (And as with so many legal issues, there may be other situations not covered here, such as what happens when there is a divorce.)

What these examples show is that every individual has different needs when it comes to legal matters. It's not one-size-fits-all, which is why consulting with an attorney to find out what your best moves are can be so vital. You don't want to find out after the fact that you neglected simple paperwork that could have spared you and your loved ones much grief.

GIFTS

Should your Power of Attorney agent be allowed to make gifts? Your first reaction might be, why should my agent be making gifts with my money to anyone? But in the legal world, the word "gift" can have implications other than giving someone a holiday present. If you own something, there may be financial consequences to that ownership. If you give it away to a family member, that could actually save you a lot of money. Sometimes keeping property until you die will have creditor or tax consequences that you can avoid by gifting the property during your lifetime. For example, if you are diagnosed with dementia and are likely to become mentally incompetent, but still might live a very long time, it may be advisable to transfer your assets.

Consider Ann and Tom, who are 65 and 68, respectively. Although Tom is mentally competent at this time, he has been diagnosed with Alzheimer's disease and is beginning to show a loss of mental capacity. Ann, whose own health is declining, knows that she will need to employ a home care worker when Tom has reached the stage where he is no longer able to handle many functions of day-to-day life. Together, Tom and Ann's total assets consist of $100,000 in joint bank accounts and $160,000 in an investment account in Tom's name alone. This couple is facing two choices. They can spend most of their hard-earned assets to pay for home care for Tom or transfer their assets to their son, Billy, and qualify for Medicaid-covered home care benefits. If Tom signs a durable POA now, his POA agent can use it to transfer the investment account to Billy at any time or when Tom's condition has deteriorated to the point where he will need home care—and at which point he would not be able to handle this transfer of assets himself.

In this example, Tom's early diagnosis gave him and his wife a warning of what was to come. But if Tom had suffered a sudden stroke that left him mentally incompetent without having executed a POA, such a transfer would not have been possible (at least not without a lengthy and costly court action).

Lawyers often encounter clients who show a great reluctance to give away their assets during their lifetime. They've spent many years working and saving and expect their children to do the same. They may feel that giving substantial assets to their children sends them the message that they do not need to work to support themselves. In addition, giving up assets seems to indicate a loss of control. But one option, discussed in Chapter Five, is transferring the assets into a Trust, which allows you to maintain some control if the Trust states that the assets cannot actually pass into the hands of your heirs until you die.

Consider the fact that the people to whom the assets will be given, such as family members, will likely inherit them anyway when you pass away. You may keep more of those assets within your family by giving them away, as opposed to paying estate taxes or spending the assets on home care or nursing home care. You'll have done yourself and your loved ones a favor by increasing their inheritance.

If Tom's condition became so severe that he could not be cared for at home, needed to be admitted to a nursing home, and sought to apply for Medicaid nursing home benefits, the POA would similarly offer him the opportunity of preserving some if not all of his assets in order to qualify. Without the POA, he and his family might be forced to spend most of his assets.

Warning: Medicaid laws are very complicated and differ from state to state. Moreover, those Medicaid regulations that govern home care coverage and nursing home coverage differ greatly. Therefore, you are urged to consult with an experienced attorney in your state before transferring your assets and applying for Medicaid benefits.

These decisions can be complicated, which is one major reason why you'd want to use an attorney both to advise you about the type of POA that would be best for you and to prepare a POA that would be accepted by financial institutions. POAs are state specific, and each state has its own acceptable form, so if it is not properly drafted, the random POA form you printed off the web may be worthless. You should also consult an attorney with regard to all other issues affecting your plans for the future, especially the potential tax consequences of making gifts. Should you be unable to act for yourself at the required time, you'll have many more planning options if you include wording in your durable POA that allows your POA agent to make gifts.

The tax laws with regard to making gifts can be quite complicated, but an attorney can guide you through the maze of these laws and steer you toward decisions that will yield the best results in terms of limiting or eliminating taxes.

DOES THE PERSON WHO IS YOUR HCP AGENT NEED TO BE YOUR POA AGENT?

Selecting who should serve as your POA agent takes some thought. Let's say you have a niece who is a nurse. She'd make the most sense as your HCP agent as she'd understand what the doctors were saying. But since your son is an accountant, you might want him to be your POA agent. Of course, there are many situations in which you'd want the same person on both documents. So the answer to this question, as with so many others, is "it depends." Being able to ask such questions of someone who's guided many clients and knows the possible pitfalls is why it really pays to seek the advice of an elder law attorney.

There may be advantages to having one person be your POA agent and another be your health care agent, as this example demonstrates:

An older man who has severe health problems has two sons, one of whom lives in his town and another who lives far away. The son who lives close by is the agent responsible for the father's physical care, and the son who lives far away is his POA agent. That POA agent son is able to handle all the financial matters, thus lessening the burden on his brother, as well as making himself feel a lot less stressed for not being there.

POAs AND TRUSTS

The subject of Trusts is a complicated one which is discussed further in the next chapter, but the benefits often make the cost and effort worthwhile. There are many reasons to use a Trust in estate planning, including eliminating the need for a complex, lengthy, and expensive probate court process, controlling the distribution of assets to your intended beneficiaries with minimal interference by others, maximizing estate tax exemptions, and qualifying for Medicaid or other forms of governmental financial assistance. It is always advisable to consult with an attorney who specializes in estate planning or elder law to guide you through the entire planning process.

If all your assets are owned by a Trust and therefore managed by a trustee, do you still need to name someone as your agent in a POA? The answer is yes; you need both, as each document is used for different purposes. The tasks needed to be performed by your agent under a POA may have nothing to do with managing your Trust assets. Your agent under a POA may be required to file your personal income taxes, sign contracts, apply for nursing home or home care benefits, and manage your retirement accounts. The role of the trustee is to manage and distribute the assets in your Trust according to your instructions. Your trustee and your POA agent can be the same person or different persons.

SOME PROTECTIVE TERMS YOU CAN ADD TO YOUR POA

A POA may include restrictive language that clearly expresses your wishes and sets limits. For example, it could state that your agent must keep precise records and that these records must be shown either to you, if that is possible, or to someone else you designate, such as a monitor. (In some states record keeping by a POA agent is mandatory, and there is a movement to make it mandatory nationwide.) When asking for any such records kept by your POA agent, make sure to do it in writing and keep a copy of the letter. If you have suspicions that your agent has been acting in an inappropriate manner, then send this letter so that you get a signed receipt, such as by certified mail. If you end up having to go to court to try to get back money that you feel your agent has misspent, having a paper trail will give more credence to your case than saying that you asked for an accounting verbally. A written request will also give you proof of exactly when you asked for this accounting so that any transactions negotiated by the agent after the fact might look all the more suspicious.

In some states, you may also name more than one person to be your Power of Attorney agent. Other states do not permit this. If you have two children, you can name both and decide whether they need to act together or whether only one of them can sign documents such as withdrawal slips and checks. If you require two people to act together, this would serve as a check on each of the agents. Of course having two agents could result in conflicts between them, as well as making for a generally more complex arrangement, as they must always act in unison. The POA could also include instructions for resolving disputes. Another possibility is to have the two agents act in sequence, so that one is really the primary agent, but if he or she wasn't around the other could fill in.

A POA is a powerful tool. You should exercise a great deal of caution in choosing a person to act as your POA agent.

Another option is to appoint different agents for different purposes. For example, if you were going to be unavailable to sign documents for the sale of your house on a certain date, you could appoint a limited agent for only this purpose whose powers expire by a certain date. You need to discuss all these options with your attorney.

Why do you need to concern yourself about such limitations? A POA is a powerful tool. If the agent you appoint is not entirely trustworthy or even just careless, the POA could be misused and your trust abused. You may have heard the terms *de jure* and *de facto*. These are Latin terms used in law. *De jure* means "by law" and *de facto* means "by fact." Legally speaking, your agent isn't allowed to empty your bank account to pay off his gambling debts. That is clearly against the law. If your agent did that, you could go to court and sue to get your money back. But if the agent steals from you using the POA and there isn't a penny left when you or your family discover the theft, there's not much that can be done about it. So *de jure* you've got the law on your side, but *de facto* you're without much recourse. That's why you have to be very careful about whom you choose to be your agent.

If you're extra cautious, and perhaps rightfully so, you could have the POA drafted and signed but keep it in your possession or maybe with your lawyer. Then, when the agent is needed, he or she could be called upon and given the POA. By holding back delivery of the POA to the agent, at least you'd know that the powers you'd granted couldn't be used until the POA document was in your agent's hands. If you choose not to deliver your POA to your agent until you think you need to make use of it, make sure you do not place the document beyond the reach of your agent, like in a bank vault, or forget where you have hid it. Tell someone where it is in the event you become incapacitated. The POA will do you no good if it cannot be located when it is needed.

You could choose a professional you already have a relationship with to handle your financial matters, such as an accountant, financial advisor, or lawyer. But these individuals may be reluctant to take on this sensitive and personal task, and if they do agree to do so they will likely charge you for their services. If the job becomes time consuming, the cost may be more than you can afford. While a family member or friend might receive some compensation, it won't amount to what a professional would likely charge.

One way of adding a layer of protection is to notify others— family members, friends, or professionals like an accountant—that you've signed a POA and named your agent. Let them know your intentions. If you become incapacitated and one of these people thought that the person you appointed was misusing the POA, they could challenge the POA legally, hopefully before too much damage was done.

By the way, if your POA is old, it may be time to update it, not just because you want to change the agent or the terms, but because many states have updated their forms over the years. While this may not mean that your old POA is invalid, an outdated version of the document may add a layer of complication at the time it is needed. Of course if your needs have changed, you should review the actual powers given by the POA and make any necessary revisions.

GIVING UP CONTROL

Many people absolutely refuse to consider signing a POA because they are afraid of giving up any control over their financial matters. They fear that doing so will allow the person they name as their agent to snoop into their financial records or perhaps rob them behind their back. Keeping secrets from a spouse is not that uncommon, is it? The person they would likely make their agent is more often than not a close relative, a spouse, a son or daughter whom they love, but still this doesn't seem to allay their basic fear. The idea of giving up control is just too scary. If the relative being named agent had a criminal record, this fear might be justified. But even parents who have absolute confidence in their offspring will often come down with a serious case of "Fear of POA."

When it comes to POAs, there are two opposing concerns: the trouble caused by not having a POA versus the fear that a POA will be abused. So how do you navigate these tricky waters? Taking an assessment of the risks that you face is part of the answer. But before you begin that analysis, you need to know a bit more about POAs.

First, the HCP that was described in the previous chapter is a type of POA. In fact, as mentioned, in some states it's called a Healthcare POA. As you've read, an HCP is limited in scope, only covering matters of your health *when you are incapacitated.* As long as you're of sound mind and can make your own decisions, your HCP agent cannot make these decisions. That's not necessarily true of a POA, of which there are different types. Sometimes, even though you are capable of handling your affairs, it may not be convenient to do so. For example, perhaps you are selling out-of-state property and are unable to travel to be present at the closing of sale. You could then appoint someone through a POA, limited in scope for just that one purpose or transaction, to act on your behalf.

CONCLUSION

After reading about Powers of Attorney and the possible dangers or abuses associated with them, you might conclude that, given the risks, that this is a document you don't need. It's true that, unfortunately, there are people without a conscience who use their power as an agent to prey on others. In spite of this limited risk, more often than not POAs prove to be lifesavers. Failing to make a POA without considering all the advantages of having one is a big mistake.

The most important decision in drafting a POA is to choose the right agent. If you have at least one person in your life whom you can trust implicitly, then you won't have any potential problems with a POA. If everyone who comes to mind has more minuses than pluses, then maybe the better decision might be not to appoint anyone as your agent. But this applies to just a small portion of 55-year-olds. The vast majority of people would be well served to have a durable POA to protect them if they are unable to act for themselves.

AN ADDITIONAL EXAMPLE

In our practices, POAs have been used to sell out-of-state property no longer in use, transfer funds from one bank account to another, pay day-to-day living expenses, make investment decisions, pay back taxes, transfer primary homesteads to joint owners to avoid nursing home liens, represent a disabled person in a lawsuit, renew a health or life insurance policy that had lapsed, obtain medical records, and resolve creditor claims with medical providers and hospitals. As we said earlier, lawyers see examples of why POAs are so necessary on a regular basis. Hopefully, we've convinced you of that, but in case you remain undecided, here is one more example of what can go wrong and how a POA can be of service:

> *Joanne's client, Donna, was an elderly childless widow with substantial assets. Donna knew that her single older brother, John, made her the sole beneficiary of his $500,000 estate in his Will. John's Will also provided that their nieces and*

nephews would receive his estate if Donna predeceased him. Because Donna had substantial assets, she was advised that her estate would have to pay a hefty estate tax upon her death. She she did not need her brother's inheritance and did not want her estate to have the burden of paying additional estate tax. Moreover, she wanted her inheritance from John to go instead to their nieces and nephews. She knew she could assure this would happen if she refused or "disclaimed" her share of his estate if he died first.

Luckily, Donna had executed a Durable POA naming her good friend, Pam, to act for her. She had told Pam that she wanted the nieces and nephews, the "kids" as she called them, to get John's estate assets. By the time John died, Donna no longer had the capacity to make her own decisions. But her wishes were carried out by Pam, who used her agency authority under the POA to disclaim Donna's share of John's estate. The result of this disclaimer by Donna's POA agent was that Donna's share of John's estate went instead to the "kids." This favorable result, a tax saving and bequest to the next generation, was made possible by a durable POA and Donna's responsible POA agent.

The important lesson here is that, beyond saving on taxes, a Durable POA can be very useful in any number of circumstances, many of them unpredictable. Having this important document in place just in case can ease stress and emotional turmoil. The only way to ensure that your loved ones can act in your best interest quickly and effectively is for you to give them the authority to do so by appointing one or more of them as your agent in a POA.

CHAPTER FIVE

Document 4: Wills, Trusts, and Other Planning Tools

A Will is a document that states your wishes as to who will inherit your assets and how they will be distributed after you have passed away.

Wills are probably the best-known legal document. They have a long history of use and have played a dramatic role in history, movie plots, and television shows. Many people believe that right after a death, if the deceased left a Will, there is a "reading" at which the family appears in the lawyer's office to finally learn what they're getting. The moment is portrayed with great suspense. But does this ever really happen today? No, because a Will isn't accepted as valid until a special type of court—called a probate court or a surrogate's court—confirms its validity and appoints an estate representative, called an executor, to follow the instructions in the Will. Certain strict formalities have to be followed for a Will to be deemed a valid last Will and the rules and procedures are different in each state.

The late comedian Henny Youngman used to tell a joke about the reading of the Will: "Old man Krastenfeld lay on his deathbed for months and finally passed away. Two weeks later, the relatives gathered like vultures to hear the reading of the Will. The lawyer tore open an envelope, drew out a piece of paper, and read: 'Being of sound mind, I spent every dime before I died.'"

Some people think that a Will is only for the wealthy who want to save on estate taxes, which is an important benefit for some people. But the primary reason to make a Will is to leave your assets to those you care about in the manner and in the amounts you choose. Statistics show that a majority of Americans don't have a Will. There may be a number of reasons for this. First, a Will forces you to face your death. This is a subject that many people would prefer not to think about. Another reason is that a Will is not a simple document to prepare. You can do it cheaply with some online form, but the process may leave you with more questions than answers, such as who should manage my estate and to whom do I give my assets? What will happen if the person to whom I give my assets dies before me? Using a lawyer to advise you and draw up your Will costs money, and these funds need to be spent long before the Will itself will have an effect. So while many "Will-less" people know they need one, they keep deferring this process for a later date as the benefits seem remote. You have to pay now, but you may personally never experience any benefit other than peace of mind, so sadly and often a Will never gets done.

> **Because estate planning involves thoughts about death, it is a subject most people prefer not to think about.**

Dying isn't as easy as it looks. While your death may put a period on your life on earth, there will most definitely be consequences for those close to you who survive you. We all leave something behind, and how your assets get passed on will be determined exclusively by state law unless you write a Will stating your wishes. Making a Will is part of what is called "estate planning." This means that you have made plans for what happens to what you own—your "estate"—after your death. Estate planning can also potentially save your heirs quite a bit of money. There may be state and/or federal taxes due, depending on your state of residence, the persons you leave your estate to, and the value of your estate when you die. These can be reduced or avoided with proper estate planning. If you do not have much in the way of assets to leave your family, you may think it is not important to have a Will. But if you die with an estate of a few thousand dollars, it is likely to be more expensive to pass on this amount without a Will than with one. And if you die with little more than the personal items in your home, even if it is not necessary to bring your Will to the court for probate, the Will may serve as a guide for the distribution of your things, including in some states your personally owned vehicle. If for no other reason, a Will can serve to keep peace among your heirs by removing any doubt about your wishes. With the guidance of an attorney, you may even explain why you made certain decisions in your Will to limit the questions asked.

Many Americans own a home which may have substantial value, so even if your bank accounts and savings are modest, your estate could be sizable because of the value of your house. Personal property, with its often sentimental or family value, also needs to be distributed. A clear plan to give away special items can go a long way in maintaining family harmony and providing solace to loved ones. Once you're deceased there's nothing you can do about a disagreement about who gets what because of your lack of planning. So in addition to possibly eliminating or lowering the tax burden on your family, if you plan ahead you may also avoid potential family strife. If you fail to make a Will, your heirs may inherit a major headache.

DYING WITHOUT A WILL

If you die without a Will, you've died "intestate." So what happens to your property? You give up your chance to decide who gets what since you didn't spell out your wishes in a Will. So who does receive your estate? If you die without a Will, the state in which you resided upon your death decides the distribution of your assets according to its "intestate distribution" law. Your property will likely pass according to strict bloodlines. For example, if you are married with children, your spouse may not inherit your entire estate and part of your estate may go directly to your children. These laws can be quite complicated and often dictate a division of property that does not match up with a person's wishes to give their estate to the persons they love and are closest to. In many states, for example, if you die without a spouse, children, parents, brothers or sisters, or nieces and nephews, your first cousins get your estate, with one-half of your assets going to your first cousins on your mother's side of the family and one-half going to your first cousins on your father's side. If these persons cannot be easily located or live abroad, your estate can be tied up in court for years. Things are likely to get more complicated, expensive, and time-consuming if one of those first cousins is a child, is unable to consent to the court process due to disability, or dies before he or she gets his or her share of your estate. Is that something you really want to happen? And what if your children are minors or your spouse needs the money? While you may say that you have no intentions of dying anytime soon, if you're honest with yourself you know that it's not under your control. But you *do* have control over what happens to your assets, if you write a Will.

Here's something else to consider if you die without a Will and leave behind young children or grandchildren. If any of your children or grandchildren are under 18 at the time of your death, in many states, if not all, the court will require the appointment of a guardian to manage the minor child's share of your assets. Although the surviving parent of the child has a good chance of being named guardian of the minor child's property, this is not guaranteed. Further, the guardian of a minor child may have to post a bond. Bond premiums can be costly. Courts usually require guardians to file annual accountings and obtain court permission before assets can be used to pay for a child's living costs, education, and medical expenses. These tasks, which can be a costly and time-consuming proposition, can be avoided with a properly drafted Will.

In addition, it is especially important that you make a Will that provides for what is called a "guardian of the person," or personal guardian, for your child in the event you and your child's other parent die at the same time. A guardian of the person may be named in your Will. Generally, a court will confirm your wishes if the person you named in your Will is found suitable to care for your child. Failing this, the court will choose a guardian for your child if he or she has no surviving parent. A guardian of the person is given custody of your child until her or his legal adulthood. You may choose one person as a property guardian and another person as a personal guardian of your minor child. Above all, if you die leaving young children with no living parent, would you not want to choose the person or persons who will continue to raise and support them? If you are a single parent of minor children it is all the more important that you make a Will that appoints guardians and alternate guardians. This will ensure, as best you can, that in the event of your death, loving people who know your children's needs will be permitted to assume responsibility for them.

As you can see, the consequences of not having a Will can be quite serious in many circumstances. Here's one example, and as you'll see, the woman who died was far from reaching 55:

Mary was in her mid-30s when she tragically died in a car accident on her way home from work one afternoon. Her distraught husband, Matt, was suddenly left with the full responsibility of caring for their two young children, ages 4 and 6. The family home was jointly held by Mary and Matt, but Mary had three bank accounts in her name alone and several small custodial accounts for her children for which Mary was named sole custodian. The total funds in all these accounts was under $100,000. So now in addition to mourning for his wife, taking care of his children, and looking for child care help at home so he could go to work to support his family, Matt had to apply to the court to become administrator of his wife's estate in order to access her assets. Then, Matt needed to make another court application to be named successor custodian on his wife's custodial accounts for the children. But before he could do any of this, he needed to make a third court application to be appointed legal guardian of his children's property. It all seemed so unnecessary, but worst of all, it cost him thousands of dollars and one year to accomplish all this due to numerous court delays.

What was most upsetting for this heart-broken father was that he had to go through a background check to be screened for criminal activity, including child abuse, before the courts would approve the application for his appointment as guardian. Moreover, he must continue to report to the court annually for the funds he holds for the benefit of his children until they are aged 18.

If Mary and Matt had consulted with a lawyer they each would have made Wills leaving all their assets to the other, or at least been advised to each list the other as a joint owner on all bank accounts. They might have been further advised to list each other as an alternate custodian on their children's custodian accounts. Substantial stress and added expense at an already impossibly difficult time could have been averted. Had Mary and Matt's estate been properly planned, none of what he went through would have occurred.

Here is another example of what can happen when one fails to make a will or other estate plan:

At age 70, Diane, a retired executive secretary for a wealthy investment advisor, who never married or had any children, died in New York City. Despite always intending to get around to it, she never made a Will. Diane, who had lived a frugal life in order to save for her old age, owned a modest one-family home and had about $500,000 in cash assets. She had been generous with only one person in her life, her cousin Mark, often paying his rent and giving him regular spending money to make ends meet. Diane told Mark that she would always take care of him and leave him most of her estate.

Diane's next of kin consisted of her mother, Sylvia, age 99, who suffered from advanced dementia and lived in another state, and one niece, Anna, the daughter of her only sibling, her deceased sister, Eve. Sadly, niece Anna suffered from drug dependency and had already squandered her share of her mother Eve's estate.

Under the intestate, or "no will," laws of New York state, Diane's entire estate went to her mother, Sylvia, who herself died intestate within two years of Diane's death, but before Diane's estate assets were paid to her. As a result of Diane's failure to make a Will, her estate assets took nearly four years to wind through the courts of two states before they were given to niece Anna, Sylvia's only living grandchild. Court proceedings were delayed because a guardian had to be appointed for Sylvia in connection with Diane's estate proceeding because Sylvia was unable to represent her own interests due to her disability.

Unfortunately, as a result of the delay in accessing funds, Diane's house was completely neglected, resulting in the heat being shut off and the house suffering major damage from burst water pipes. Diane's failure to plan resulted in a huge waste of resources and resulted in all of her estate assets being given outright to Anna. If Diane had made a Will, she might have given some of her assets to her cousin, Mark, and left some of her assets in Trust for the benefit of her niece, Anna. Years of delay, unnecessary court applications, and legal fees could have been avoided.

We can all count on the fact that life is uncertain. Life can change and tumble our world upside in a moment or slowly over years. The next example shows how badly matters can turn out when a family tries to take care of legal matters without consulting a lawyer:

An elderly couple owned a two-family house that they had scrimped and saved over a lifetime to buy and maintain. It was their only asset, other than a small checking account. Jared, one of their three sons, lived in the second-floor apartment and the parents lived on the first floor. Since he took care of the house and of them, the couple went to a lawyer they knew and transferred the title of their home to Jared. Jared agreed that when his parents passed away he would sell the house and divide up the sales proceeds with his brothers.

Jared then got married, and his father became very ill and ended up in a nursing home. Within one year, Jared passed away suddenly. He didn't have a Will. This meant that the parents' house now belonged to the Jared's widow. And since the widow didn't get along with her in-laws, she brought a court proceeding to evict her mother-in-law from the home! The two surviving sons faced the loss of the inheritance that the parents wanted all their sons to share.

The idea of transferring the house was a good one, but a simple transfer to one son was not the way to go. This family should have been guided to take steps to assure that the parents were protected during life and that their estate would go equally to the three sons after death. Sadly, these protections were never even considered. The house could have been put in a Trust that would have protected the parents' rights. Or at the very least, Jared should have prepared a Will at the time the deed was transferred to protect the interests of his parents and brothers. Although not an absolute protection, this would have gone a long way toward ensuring the proper transfer of the proceeds resulting from the sale of the house. Of course, no one expected this healthy young man to predecease his parents, but the unexpected is exactly what people need to be protected from.

DOMESTIC PARTNERS

Fewer people are marrying these days. And even if two people plan to eventually marry, nobody thinks twice about cohabitating beforehand, so there are more households where two people live together but have no legal ties. What that means is if one of them passes away, the other has absolutely no legal title to any of the other's assets, including a shared home that is owned by one of them.

If it is your wish that your unmarried partner or your friend inherit your assets and you do not have a valid Will that directs that your assets be given to him or her, this person may be left out in the cold, literally. This is what happened to Sam:

One of our clients, Mario, owned a home in which he lived with his romantic partner, Sam, for thirty years. When they were in their 60s, Mario died. Mario, who loved Sam and intended for

Sam to live in the home for the rest of his life, never made a Will that gave Sam this right. As a result, Mario's three sisters were legally entitled to the house. Of course, the sisters wished to cash out their shares by selling the house as soon as possible. Sam was forced to move out of his home, and he received no part of Mario's estate except for the $10,000 they had in a joint bank account. After the expensive move to a new place, Sam was "out in the cold" and virtually penniless.

If Mario had created a Will, he could have protected his beloved partner in one of many ways by leaving him the house, leaving Sam the lifetime right to live in the house, or giving him part or all of the proceeds from the sale of the house.

The above example is extreme, but tragic tales like this one are often shared by the clients who call on us for help. As attorneys we are often consulted too late, at a point when we and our client are powerless to change things. Putting aside real estate, which often is quite valuable, sometime money is not what is most important to people following the loss of a loved one. Just because an item doesn't have much monetary value doesn't mean that it doesn't have real value. You may have inherited your grandmother's wedding ring. The gold is worn thin so its value is mostly sentimental, but shouldn't you decide who is the right person to wear it next?

It's true that younger people don't die as often as older people, but that's not to say it never happens. If all two people share are some second-hand furniture and a set of dishes, then it doesn't matter. But if they have any assets of significant value together, maybe a new car they bought or two weeks in a timeshare, then a way to make sure that ownership of the asset goes to the person or persons they want to inherit it is through a Will.

As we said in the beginning of this book, 55 is the age when estate matters become more time sensitive and the odds of procrastination causing harmful effects increase. But no matter your age (and some of you reading this book may be doing so thinking that it applies only to your parents), carefully examining the need for legal protection is something everyone should do periodically.

WILL PLANNING: THE FIRST STEP

In many instances, people who don't have a Will also don't have a reliable inventory of exactly what they own. They have only a vague idea of the entirety of the assets that make up their estate. This can leave their family in chaos as they scramble to identify and distribute the assets. So the first step in planning a Will just involves you and doesn't cost a cent. Put together a list of all the information about your estate and your assets—a financial and legal outline (you'll be asked for this at an initial meeting with a lawyer). At a minimum, for each asset you should list how title to the asset is held, meaning whether the asset is held by you alone or with others, whether the asset has a named beneficiary, and its current value. You should describe each item carefully and include any additional relevant information; for example, whether the asset is owned subject to a loan or someone has some other rights to the property, such as the right to legally occupy a house. Putting in the effort

The first step in planning a Will just involves you and doesn't cost a cent.

of assembling all this information will undoubtedly lead you to follow through and make a Will, but even if it doesn't motivate you to do so, organizing the puzzle that is your life is a useful exercise.

So exactly what do you need? Your lawyer can provide an estate planning questionnaire for you to use to plan for your Will. (For an example of such a questionnaire, see Appendix A: Client Questionnaire.) If you are prepared with the necessary asset information, the creation of your Will will go faster and more efficiently for you, your family, and your attorney.

Often, lawyers charge an inclusive flat fee for preparing documents like Wills or Trusts. If a client is indecisive and uses up a great deal of time by not being prepared, changing his or her mind all the time, and so on, then the lawyer may charge additional fees. The documents helpful in creating a complete picture of your estate include:

- Drivers license/passport (for identity)
- Social Security card (for tax records)

- Personal income tax returns for the previous two years
- Wills, Health Care Proxies, and Living Wills if already executed and which may need to be amended
- Name, address, telephone number, and email address of your accountant and/or financial advisor
- Deeds for real estate/co-operative apartment unit documents (stock certificate and lease)
- Corporate or company information, business documents, like shares of stock or other forms of ownership including agreements between co-owners
- Annuity/retirement accounts/IRA/pension information
- Most recent bank statements for all accounts
- Life insurance policy/cash value and beneficiary(ies)
- Brokerage account statements
- Stock certificates/Treasury notes, bonds, and bills
- Mortgage papers (payment book)
- Real estate tax bills for any real estate

Now if you're cautious you may say to yourself, I don't want someone else, even a lawyer I'm paying, to know so much about my affairs. That's an understandable reaction, but the irony is that your unwillingness to provide your lawyer with information and precise details about your estate assets, next of kin, and other facts unique to your situation can lead to the opposite outcome. If you don't have a Will after you die, your estate is more likely to end up in court in order to sort everything out. So instead of talking to a lawyer, in private, who is required by law to keep your information and secrets in strict confidence (unless you authorize her to disclose them), your family could end up in court, in a public proceeding with a public record, and your well-guarded privacy may then become a thing of the past. Does that sound preferable?

If you need any concrete proof that court proceedings are public record, just read the newspapers after a celebrity like Brooke Astor or James Gandolfini passes away. (To protect yourself from this type of disclosure, you might consider placing your assets in a Trust.) But even if you are not famous, you might end up in the papers. Lawyers are sometimes ordered by the court to place ads in newspapers in cities, even some in other countries, where any distant relatives of yours might live in order to announce your death so that they have the opportunity to come forward and participate in your estate proceeding.

On the other hand, when Robin Williams passed away, there was no easy way for the press or anyone else to learn what was in his estate because his assets were left in a Trust, and Trusts are not required to be filed in the public records of a court. A Trust will keep the details of your estate private (which is often important to celebrities), whereas a Will becomes a public court record. Williams wanted to protect his privacy, and his lawyers were able to provide him the privacy he desired. Of course, this did not stop his family from squabbling over personal items and memorabilia, even though it appears that Williams was a careful planner.

Keep in mind that any client has to cooperate with their lawyer's suggested plan to achieve a successful result. Sometimes lawyers set up a Trust for a client and then the client fails to follow the agreed upon instructions and place his or her assets into the Trust, which defeats the purpose of creating the Trust in the first place. Even the use of a clear, well drafted Trust to transfer your assets does not assure that your plan will not be challenged, but Trust planning is often more private and can make a challenge less likely.

If you have a well-written, well-planned Will or Trust, prepared by a lawyer and signed in the manner required by law, then your property will likely be passed from you to your intended beneficiaries smoothly and according to your wishes. But if you don't have a Will or Trust, or if the Will or Trust is not clear, then the likely outcome **Lawyers know how to anticipate pitfalls.** could be chaos. That may sound like an exaggeration, and if all your family members are perfectly rational and never argue, then the process would only be a bit overwhelming. But what lawyers see, over and over again, is the shattering of family unity as factions develop and unearth family issues that should have been buried with their dearly departed! There may even be all-out war because there is no clear direction from the decedent.

Again, if there is no Will or Trust, the distribution of estate assets follows strict formulas established by state law. (Though state laws for the distribution of an estate are all similar, each state has its own differences as well.) So even though one daughter may have taken care of Mom for the last twenty years while her siblings never even visited, all the siblings will get an equal share, whether that seems "fair" or not.

Another problem that may arise (and here we must repeat that each state has slightly different laws so the following is not an exact description of the procedures followed by the courts in your state) is that an executor, who may be called an administrator if there is no Will, must be appointed. Again, if the family members all get along, this can be an easy decision, but if they don't, then who is selected to fill this role may be something to fight over. And administrators of an estate without a Will don't have the same powers as executors when there is a Will. An administrator is usually more closely supervised by the court, and may have to return to court to get permission to proceed with various administrative duties, like the selling of property. The administrator may also have to be bonded. All these court appearances usually mean that the process of distributing the estate will take much longer than if there is a Will.

And while the distribution of property that can be easily sold, such as a house or stock portfolio that can be broken down into equal shares, may be accomplished without difficulty, that may not be true with respect to all the deceased's personal belongings, some of which may have sentimental value over and above what they may be worth financially. Grandma's engagement ring, for example, which has been in the family for many years, could simply be sold and the proceeds divided, but then it would lose its status as a family heirloom that is treasured as it is passed from generation to generation. But if family members can't agree on who gets it, then its sale becomes more likely. And this can happen whether there is no Will or if there is a Will, but it fails to include instructions about who gets personal property.

Family members who've gotten along for decades, faced with the potential of having a greater inheritance or finally getting the hand-embroidered bedcover from Grandma's bed, may turn on one another and underlying conflicts may emerge. It seems irrational, but it happens. Long-buried family rivalries and sibling feuds that have been simmering in the background rekindle. Facing the death of a loved one is very difficult, even when everyone gets along. Why make it worse by leaving confusing instructions or no instructions at all about how your assets will be distributed? You don't want to leave your family in tatters just because you happened to pass away. Your Will or testamentary plan can provide a clear and legally defensible road map for the family to follow, and save your loved ones from the strife of all these pitfalls.

CAUTION, DO NOT TRY AT HOME: THE SELF-MADE WILL

What if you decide to buy a form online and make out your own Will? It's certainly a cheaper solution, but will it be an effective one?

A lawyer told us about a woman who on her own wrote out a Will that said her assets were to be divided among her heirs when her investments had reached a certain sum. She died, the stock market went down, and instead of rising, her investments were sinking. Because the assets might never reach the goal she'd set, they might never be passed on to her heirs. The more time passed the lower the value went, so her heirs had to hire a lawyer in an attempt to overturn the terms of the Will. Those legal fees cost far more than what it would have cost the woman to hire an attorney to make a Will that made sense.

And here's a case in which a Florida Supreme Court judge got involved:

A woman used an EZ legal form to draft her Will. Later on, her sister predeceased her, leaving her a gift that ended up falling outside the Will because it wasn't covered in the EZ form. The

Will was then contested and the case went all the way to the Florida Supreme Court. In the court's March 2014 ruling, the Florida justice noted that the simple Will intended to save money wound up in costly litigation. The court noted that the case served to "to highlight a cautionary tale of the potential dangers of utilizing pre-printed forms and drafting a Will without legal assistance." You see, most judges are overloaded with cases, and there's nothing they want less than to see their dockets filled with cases that could have been avoided if the people involved had consulted with a lawyer rather than a computer!

Lawyers know how to anticipate pitfalls. It's not that the women in these two instances couldn't have made Wills that stated their wishes. But a lawyer would have made sure that there was also language that would have protected the first woman's property if circumstances were such that her wishes couldn't be met because of falling stock prices. Can lawyers foresee every problem? Maybe not, but an experienced estate planning lawyer who knows the pitfalls is going to be a good investment and will ensure that you avoid most if not all of them.

SHARED PROPERTY

If you have a joint bank account with your spouse (or anyone else for that matter) when one of you passes away, the entire sum in the account belongs to the other party, the joint owner. That's also true of real property when both your names are listed as joint owners on a deed. But what if you and your spouse die together in a traffic or plane accident? Owning some of your assets jointly can replace the need for a Will for those joint assets because they designate the survivor as the owner. But when there is no survivor, the problem remains. Joint ownership is not a cure-all.

If you have an insurance policy, the beneficiary of the policy will receive the funds because the policy names an individual to receive the proceeds. Thus an insurance policy falls outside the directions made in a Will. The same can be true for pension benefits, IRAs, or annuities, which are not governed by a Will as long as they name beneficiaries. If the beneficiary is your estate, or you fail to name a beneficiary, then the money flows into your estate according to the terms of your 401k accounts, other retirement accounts, and annuities.

A spouse has special inheritance protections. If you do not want your spouse to get any assets that you own, you may not be able to accomplish this, even if you make a specific Will leaving your spouse nothing. In many states, a surviving spouse can't be completely disinherited and has the right to "elect against the Will," that is to say, to challenge the disinheritance in order to receive a partial inheritance. Children, on the other hand, have no specific right to an inheritance and can be written out of a Will.

IN TERROREM CLAUSE

In Latin, *in terrorem* means "in fear." The *in terrorem* clause is designed to put fear into those named as beneficiaries of a Will so that they won't challenge it. This clause basically says that anyone who is a beneficiary under a Will who challenges any of the provisions of that Will will be disinherited or given a nominal fee. Another name for this is the "no-contest" clause. Of course, not all of these clauses are only a clause long. The no-contest clause in Frank Sinatra's Will went on for pages, outlining any possible situation that might be interpreted as an attack against the Will.

Having such a clause doesn't guarantee that potential heirs won't sue, it just creates a deterrence. If you leave one child the bulk of your estate and the other a few hundred dollars, the second child might figure she has nothing much to lose by challenging the Will. Of course that second child will likely need to invest significant money and time in such a contest and may well lose much more than a few hundred dollars.

W. C. Fields had a no-contest clause in his Will that left no inheritance to his estranged wife. He wanted his estate to benefit the W. C. Fields College for Orphans, but his wife objected after his death. Because he'd never officially divorced his wife, when she challenged his Will she won, and the college never received Fields's bequest. The no-contest clause was ineffective.

Every state looks at these clauses differently. The Uniform Probate Code (UPC), which sets a national standard for Wills, permits for no-contest clauses, but also states that such clauses may be challenged if there is a good reason for such a challenge. Many states have adopted the rules for Wills found in the UPC. Other states have chosen to draw up their own rules regarding these clauses. In some states, such as Florida, the no-contest clause is unenforceable. Other states will enforce such clauses with exceptions. In New York, for example, there is an exception allowing a minor to contest a Will on the grounds of forgery or revocation by a later Will.

Sometimes a particular part of a Will can be challenged without invoking the no-contest clause. Michael Jackson's mother asked a judge if she could challenge the choice of executor of Michael's Will, under which she stood to inherit $40 million, without activating this clause. The judge ruled in her favor.

The most common reason Wills are challenged are in situations where one adult child assumes the full care of a parent and the Will then leaves a much larger share to that child. The other adult children feel that their sibling exerted undue influence to induce the parent to give the caretaker child more of the estate. They do not accept that their parent simply thought that such a division was fairer given how much more care the one child gave over the parent's lifetime. This is a story that experienced estate attorneys hear again and again.

The best way to avoid fights between heirs when leaving differing amounts is to speak to them about this before you pass away. While they may not like your decision, hearing it from your mouth will make it less likely that they will challenge the Will later on. Another way to do this is to describe the reason for the unequal division in the Will itself. If heirs will not listen to reason, then a no-contest clause might prevent a later court challenge to the Will.

A client included a $5,000 inheritance to one daughter who was hostile to the family for many years and then split the remaining estate between her two sons. The Will had a no-

contest clause. If the daughter challenged, she would lose her $5,000. This worked to deter her from causing a delay in the probate of the Will and the settlement of the estate.

Divorce can complicate matters. In some states, divorce automatically revokes the rights of the divorced spouse to inherit any assets from the ex-spouse's Will. If the divorced spouse's Will left a bequest to his ex's children from a previous marriage, those gifts would remain in the Will after a divorce, unless the terms of the Will were changed. Here's an example of what can happen:

A client, Joe, had a twenty-five-year marriage in which he treated the children of his spouse as his own. Joe's Will was a traditional "sweetheart" Will which left his entire estate to his current wife, Marie, and if not her, to Marie's children. Unfortunately, Joe and Marie divorced after twenty-five years and Joe drifted away from Marie and her children as he became involved in a new relationship. Joe eventually became more involved with his own family, specifically his nieces and nephews. He believed his divorce severed his obligation to his former wife, which their divorce decree and the state's "estate" law confirmed. Joe did not write a new Will and completely forgot he had named Marie's children in his Will. When Joe died fifteen years after his divorce, his old Will still remained, giving his estate to his ex-wife's children. His own nieces and nephews, including a disabled minor whom he had promised to provide for, received nothing.

This example highlights the need to consult an experienced lawyer and review your Will periodically, and certainly after major life changes like divorce occur.

Assuming anything when it comes to legal matters is a big mistake. In the case above, the gentleman assumed his divorce meant he didn't have to make a new Will. As it turned out, the consequences to that disabled nephew were severe.

THE ROLE OF THE EXECUTOR

One of the most important things you can do to best ensure that your estate is handled without a hitch is to appoint the right person as your executor, who is sometimes called a personal representative. A Will must name an executor to carry out your wishes. You can choose whom you would like, but know that there are many duties required of an executor that can last for a considerable amount of time, even years, depending on how complicated your estate is. So you should choose someone capable, especially when it comes to financial matters, and who has the diplomacy skills to handle any family issues that may come up.

If you can't identify anyone among your family and close friends whom you think would be capable and would agree to take on this responsibility, you can name your attorney as your executor. All executors receive a stipend, or "commission," paid from estate assets for their services. This commission is based on state law. Keep in mind that an attorney retained to perform legal work for an estate will usually charge the estate his or her normal hourly rate or take a percentage of the estate as a legal fee. This will be in addition to receiving any statutory commission he may be entitled to receive under state law. Some states require that the Will maker, called a testator, sign a special disclosure form acknowledging that she knows that her attorney may be paid both for acting as legal counsel and as executor.

If you choose someone who is going to rely on your attorney for everything, and simply show up to attach his or her signature to documents when called to do so, then your attorney will be doing most of the work in any case and charging the estate. So perhaps having your attorney act as executor could make sense, even in light of the fact that an attorney might be entitled to executor's fees as well as fees for legal work. In general, though, family members are traditionally selected as executors.

The duties of the executor are many and varied. One of the first steps an executor named in a Will must take is to arrange for his or her court appointment in a process called probate. An attorney is almost always retained to petition the court for the probate of a Will, which, if successful, results in an order appointing the executor as the person in charge of the estate. When the court appoints the executor, it issues what are commonly called "Letters Testamentary," a document that allows the executor to represent the estate to third parties such as banks and financial companies in order to collect, liquidate, and distribute assets, as well as perform many other tasks. In

Choosing the right person as your executor can ensure that your estate is handled competently and according to your wishes.

short, letters testamentary authorize the executor named in the Will to be the person in charge of the estate.

Once appointed, the executor must gather together complete information about your financial affairs. In order to simplify the burden, you should take certain steps to prepare the executor. You could review the extent and location of your assets with your executor, but if you'd prefer not to reveal your entire financial picture in advance, you could create a file that includes all the necessary estate information, alert the executor of its existence, and store it in a safe place. In addition, make sure that either your lawyer or your accountant also has complete asset information and could pass it on to your executor at the proper time. You have to be thorough about this if you want to make things as easy as possible for your executor. Sometimes people forget to list one or two assets, like a forgotten life insurance policy they had through their employer, for example. It may be for a small amount, but it still has to be counted as part of the estate and your executor won't be off the hook until everything is accounted for.

Of course, once the executor has rounded up a record of all your assets, some may need to be sold in order to be divided among those named to receive them in the Will or to pay taxes. That might include items easily sold, like stocks, and items that take a lot more time and effort to sell, such as a house or share in a business. Therefore, your executor must have some organizational skills or access to professionals to help with these tasks.

Then there are all the day-to-day details that must be handled. Credit cards must be canceled. If no family member wants to continue receiving continuous telephone and electricity service, such services may need to be discontinued, while other services might need to be continued and paid for until such time as an apartment can be emptied and turned over to a landlord. The executor must inform those utilities and cancel the accounts. Rent, taxes, and insurance premiums may need to be paid. And if there's a house that needs to be sold, then it will need to be repaired and maintained as needed and all the utilities, taxes, and hazard insurance premiums will need to be paid regularly until the sale is completed. Another troubling issue may be what to do with the car. Is it parked safely? Is the lease paid? Is the insurance up to date?

An estate bank account will have to be opened to hold collected assets so that there are funds to pay these bills and a new taxpayer ID number will be assigned to the estate. Any expenses paid will have to be carefully recorded and backed up with receipts so the executor can account for funds used to maintain the estate. Banks where the deceased person had accounts will have to be informed and funds collected into the estate account. If there is a safe deposit box, it will have to be emptied. If you were collecting Social Security or had pension payments being paid to you, the Social Security Administration and pension fund need to be notified of your death. Death benefits collected from all sources, including but not limited to IRAs and retirement accounts, will need to be turned over to their rightful beneficiaries or to the estate, as the case may be. Personal income tax returns, as well as all other local, state, and federal tax returns, must be filed for your last year of life, and then for the estate as it collects income on the assets it collects. Such estate assets can include interest income, dividends, and rental income on undistributed real estate. To some extent, being an executor is like being the sole proprietor of a short-lived business.

Some of the activities to be handled by your executor will probably require a lawyer's assistance, as stated above, such as filing the Will with the probate court. Others may require a professional accountant to handle tax filings. But the executor remains the director for that process, even if a professional will create and file all the paperwork. Ultimately, it is the executor who is responsible and accountable for the collection of assets, the payment of all estate expenses, debts, and taxes, and finally the distribution of assets according to the Will.

Because there is so much to do and estate beneficiaries are dependent on the executor's actions, you must choose your executor carefully and explain the duties so that your executor won't later regret having accepted taking on this role. You must also take into account the age of your executor. Normally, he or she shouldn't be someone older than you, and thus less likely to survive you. Elvis Presley chose his father, which worked out because he died at a young age, though his father did pass away only two years after Elvis. In most instances, choosing a parent will only mean that you'll have to ask someone else later on, and not only because a parent is more likely to die before you, but also because the odds of a parent becoming incapable in some manner by the time you pass away are also much greater.

If you've chosen someone your own age, you may later want to change your executor if you find your first choice can no longer handle the necessary required duties. Depending on state regulations, your executor may also be required to reside in the same state you resided in, which is more likely if the executor is not a blood relative. Whoever you choose, it is always recommended that you name one or more alternate executors in case the first person you've named predeceases you or is not up to the job at the time of your passing.

A client named her brother, an accountant, as executor in her Will, as she did not think her only daughter was fully capable of handling the details of her estate. Her brother was eight years younger than she, and understood the nature of her assets as he had served as her financial advisor. A good choice, but two things occurred. One was positive. Sister and brother both lived well into their 80s and 90s, respectively. The other was not so great. The brother became ill and moved to Florida to live with his children. He no longer was an ideal choice for an executor as he had dementia. The client failed to name an alternate executor and did not make a new Will or amend her old Will when her brother became ill. Although her daughter was pretty inept, the client had a grandchild who was now a young, capable business executive who was willing to do the job. But the estate had to go through several steps to have the brother resign and the granddaughter appointed executor. The estate was in limbo during this delay, wasting time and money.

Amending your Will to change the executor as a result of life changes is vital. Such changes may include divorce, the death of beneficiaries, substantial changes in assets, and the birth of children.

While your executor could make mistakes in the manner in which he or she carries out the required duties, there is also the possibility that serious mistakes could occur due to an executor's failure to act or act in time. Here's one example. The federal government and each state allow you to exempt a certain value of assets from inheritance taxes. (Since this state exemption amount is subject to changes in the law and differs from state to state, we leave it unspecified, but every state either has an amount of inheritance exempt from estate tax or exempts the entire estate.) In calculating federal estate taxes, the spouse who dies can pass his or her unused exemption amount to the surviving spouse. This is called spousal "portability." However, the second spouse to die cannot take advantage of portability in order to limit taxes unless a proper and timely tax filing is made with the IRS, even though no estate taxes are due. Failure to complete this paperwork means that this benefit will not be passed on, which could result in a large tax bite when the surviving spouse dies. If the executor is working with your lawyer and accountant, the likelihood of this occurring is much less, but that's not always true. At the very least your executor needs to be asking questions to make certain that every base is covered to protect the value of your estate from unnecessary taxes and expenses. In addition, federal and most (if not all) state estate taxes must be paid within nine months of the date of death, otherwise penalties and interest are added to the amount owed. Thus, an executor may need to collect assets fairly quickly in order to access them to pay taxes.

Please note that portability—the ability to transfer the unused tax exemption between spouses—is not available in all states. Thus, a tax analysis for a decedent's state of residence must be done in addition to an analysis of federal death tax obligations. The long and short of it is that almost every estate will need to be assessed for the need to pay federal, state, and locals taxes and must pay those taxes if and when due. Death and taxes go hand in hand.

DIVIDING UP YOUR ESTATE

The bottom line of estate planning is deciding who is going to get your assets after you pass away. Even those people who studiously avoid contemplating their own death usually have feelings about whom they would like to inherit their hard-earned possessions. They would prefer to have a hand in how things turn out rather than throw the decision to fate, standardized state law, or, worse still, the courts. But when you get right down to it, figuring out "who gets what" is not always a simple process. Many factors come into play in establishing an estate plan, including fairness, the various qualities, both good and bad, of your relatives, the value of your estate assets, and the age of those who might inherit from you. Other considerations include the health, legal, and financial status of your loved ones and, let's be honest, how you want those around you to think of you after you've gone.

The last point is an important one. Let's say you have two children, one of whom has been very attentive and the other who has been mostly absent from your life. To be fair, you may want to leave the first child a bigger share than the second. But that would very likely reinforce whatever bad feelings there were between you and the second child. Is that what you want? Understanding how the division of your property will affect your relatives can color your decisions and needs to be carefully considered. Choosing who gets what is an emotional process, and your lawyer can often help you to make these choices by acting as an impartial advisor.

One way of favoring a particular person while also recognizing other familial relationships is to divide financial assets equally but give personal possessions or specific assets that pass outside the Will, such as life insurance or retirement accounts, to the person who has been closest to you by making that person the named beneficiary of these assets. Rather than disinherit anyone in your Will, it may be wise to make your point by not leaving certain items to those whom you feel are not deserving. And any gifts you make to charity can also be used to show your feelings, both in the charities you select and in the sums you give.

Speaking of gifts left to charity, these might not be a subject you should keep a secret. Considering that any money you leave to charity would otherwise go to your heirs, you should include those affected, such as your grown children, in the discussion. Even giving them some say in where a portion of the estate will go will have a positive effect on how they look at that part of your legacy. If they know that their inheritance will be reduced but have had a part in making the decision as to which charities will share your estate with them, when the time comes to make the donations, they will feel much better about the decision because it won't be a total surprise. And if your children were counting on getting the entirety of your estate while you intend to give a sizable chunk to charity, it's better they know this sooner rather than later so that they don't plan on getting money that in fact will not be forthcoming.

If you have any heirloom items, pieces that have been in your family for years or items that are particularly valuable, how these are passed on can cause a lot of friction. You may want to speak to family members before writing your Will so that you have a better understanding of who has a particular attachment to these items. Some people find this part of Will making harder than dividing up their financial assets, but if you neglect it, you'll only be passing on the difficulties to your executor. You may have very strong feelings about some of your possessions and will want them to go to someone who will feel similarly about them. John F. Kennedy, Jr. had inherited his father's collection of scrimshaw (carved, ivory figures). While he left everything to his wife, he purposefully left the scrimshaw to his sister, Caroline. And since his wife passed away with him in that horrible plane crash, if he hadn't made those arrangements, the scrimshaw might have gone to his wife's family and not remained with his.

Making these decisions can take time, especially if you opt to speak with all or many of those involved. These are not easy conversations to have. If you are hesitant to talk about your future passing, in all probability your relatives will be even less desirous of talking about that day with you. But unless you speak to them, you'll never know how they feel about, say, the grandfather clock in your living room.

And for those without any relatives to whom to pass on their estate, the process may be even more complicated. When such people pass away without a Will, their assets go to the state in which they reside. Assuming that's not what they want, then they have to decide whom to name in their Will. The inheritors could be various charities or friends or co-workers. Again, this is not a decision your lawyer can make for you, but it is one that those in this situation need to make before they consult with a lawyer to make a Will. One of the first questions a lawyer will ask is to whom are you leaving your estate? If you can't answer that question, then the entire process gets stymied.

BLENDED FAMILIES

If there is any situation that makes the creation of a Will complicated, it's the blended family—the result of divorce or death and remarriage, which often includes children from a past marriage (or several marriages) and stepchildren. This situation is one over which you must take control. If you were to die without a Will, you can be almost certain that major disagreements will arise once you're gone. But here again, making a Will forces you to make decisions about who gets what and can help you to understand the effect taxes may have on your decision making. Inheritances to spouses pass tax free. This is an inviting option, but you may want to divide your estate between your second spouse and the children of your first marriage or other relationship. A Will that uses a Trust to provide for the present spouse but preserves the remainder for your children or others can help solve some of the blended-family dilemmas.

TRUSTS FOR BLENDED FAMILIES

There are many types of Trusts and their uses serve important objectives, such as saving on taxes or providing for disabled children and present or former spouses. Trusts can be complicated, which is why this book is not going to cover them in any depth as it is meant to be a short guide and not a full explanation of every aspect of estate planning law. However, an explanation of the one type of Trust often used in blended families will serve as a good example of why you should talk with your lawyer about Trusts and discuss which ones may benefit you.

Let's say that you had divorced and remarried and wanted your new spouse to be able to maintain the lifestyle you shared together, but you also wanted your children from a previous marriage to inherit your assets once your new spouse had passed away. If you gave all your assets to your children in your Will, your new spouse could be left with nothing (or possibly only his or her spousal share under the law) and would need to depend upon the charity of your children for her support. This is awkward for both parties. But if you left your assets to your new spouse, there would be no way for you to be sure that your wishes to leave some or all of your assets to your children once your second spouse passed away would be honored. That would be especially true if your new spouse also had children from a previous marriage. Your spouse could decide to leave some, most, or all of your joint assets to her own children.

One way around this dilemma is to set up a special Trust called a "QTIP" (Qualified Terminable Interest Property) Trust. A QTIP Trust gives all the income from your assets to your new spouse to support him or her as long as that spouse lives, but passes the remainder of the Trust on to your children upon your spouse's death. Such a Trust also defers any estate tax liability until the second spouse dies, which is an example of how Trusts can be used for estate tax savings. (A QTIP Trust may also benefit traditional families and spouses.)

There is the impression that Trusts are only for rich people, and while it is true that those with high net worth can save taxes through the use of Trusts, they are useful for estates of all sizes. In estates that are likely to be subject to estate tax, highly specialized Trusts, such as Qualified Personal Resident Trusts or Grantor Retained Annuity Trusts, can be used to minimize estate taxes and meet specific needs.

People with modest estates can use Trusts to hold assets in order to qualify for Medicaid, a government program that can provide medical care, home care, or nursing home care if they have assets and income below certain financial levels. Trusts are particularly recommended for people who have complicated family dynamics that make Will contests more likely, people with real property in more than one state, and people whose beneficiaries are children or are disabled.

Jack Benny made it his stock in trade to appear as a penny-pincher, so you would expect him to attempt to save on taxes. He also used a violin in his act and owned several very valuable ones. In order to make certain that the IRS wouldn't be able to tax the value of his violins in his estate, he "donated" them to the Los Angeles Philharmonic while he was living. Since he wanted to continue to use them while alive, Benny donated them to a Living Trust that allowed him to donate only the future or remainder interest in his violins. He could keep his precious violins to use as long as he was alive, yet the violins were not part of his estate and were not taxed.

THE HIGH COST OF PLANNING TOO LATE

Trusts are often used to protect your money from being spent down for long-term care. The following case illustrates what can happen:

William, a bachelor with no living relatives, lived alone at 85. A deeply pious man, he had worked for a trucking firm for fifty years and had amassed a small fortune in stocks, bonds, and cash of almost $1 million. The trouble was that he was getting more and more confused about how to manage his life, eat well, care for himself and his tiny apartment, and keep track of *his assets after years of carefully tending to them. William had done no estate planning before he was forced to move to an assisted-living facility. After his third year living there, he was recommended to a caring lawyer. As William grew weaker, it was obvious that he would never be able to return home to live alone and would need to be transferred to a nursing home and pay upward of $13,000 per month to live there.*

Unfortunately, all of his stocks were in certificate form back in his apartment. After he had been away from his apartment for nearly two years, the place was vandalized and none of some fifty separate stock certificates were ever recovered. In order to get control over his stock so that it could be placed in a Living Trust, which would provide for any remainder after death to go to all the churches that William had loved during his lifetime, he was saddled with some $45,000 in legal, administrative, and bond fees. These fees would go to recover the lost stock certificates so his assets could be transferred to a stock management company for ease of access, investment changes, and eventual distribution to his beloved religious institutions.

If William had planned earlier and placed his assets in a Medicaid Asset Protection Trust, he could have avoided most of those legal fees. He also could have saved some of the $400,000 he spent on nursing homes because Medicaid would have picked up some of those expenses.

Is it fair to keep money outside the reach of Medicaid? Let's take the example of a husband and wife. He falls ill and has to go to a nursing home. Nursing home prices vary, but at the low end they're $5,000 a month and at the high end can be more than three times that, so a couple's savings can quickly be used up. At that point, Medicaid will pay. But now the wife falls ill. She's doesn't need to go to a nursing home, but she does need help at home, though now there's no money to pay for that. Even if the wife at home qualifies for Medicaid home care, she will need other assets and income to pay for rent, food, additional care, and other modest living expenses. Elder law attorneys can help to guide you on how you can protect your assets through Trusts and other means so that some of the savings you've built up over a lifetime can be protected.

Trusts aren't always the perfect solution; they can come with their own potential pitfalls. Trusts separate your assets from your probate estate and the control of your executor. There are always estate expenses involved when someone passes away, such as federal and state estate taxes (about one-third of the states have these), professional fees, and, of course, funeral costs. If all the assets of an estate are in a Trust, there may be no available money for the executor or estate representative to pay for these expenses. Improper planning for expenses can cause conflicts among family members or Trust beneficiaries, unless the Trust mandates the payment of estate taxes and standard estate expenses. A competent attorney will consider the coordination of the Trust with an estate and include it in an overall plan. This was the main criticism of the late James Gandolfini's Will, which required that only the probate estate pick up the tax expenses instead of spreading it across all estate and trust assets. This unfairly burdened the estate heirs and allowed the Trust heirs to escape tax liability. This result can be avoided with careful drafting.

Trusts don't go through probate, so if you wish to maintain privacy concerning your assets, you should definitely consult with an attorney about using one or more Trusts to pass on your property after you die. When a Trust creator passes away, only those who are beneficiaries of the Trust will know what assets are in the Trust and who the Trust beneficiaries are. The family of James Gandolfini might have appreciated that discretion and control instead of seeing his estate plan debated in the tabloids, on the web, and across all forms of media.

MORE PLANNING OPTIONS YOU SHOULD CONSIDER

If you'd like to donate any body parts to science, stating such a desire in your Will is not the way to do this because by the time your Will is validated by the court, your remains will be long gone.

If you wish to donate your entire body to science or specific body parts for transplant upon death, you need to carry a donor card on your person indicating such wishes. This intent should also be listed in your medical records.

Some states have a special form to direct funeral and burial arrangements. Not every state has an official form, but if you have any interest in making some or all of the decisions about your funeral, you don't want to make the mistake of putting those instructions in your Will, believing that they'll be followed. The main reason not to do this is that your Will is not binding until it has been approved by a probate or surrogate's court, which can take time. However, your funeral is likely to take place immediately or soon after your death. For this reason, leaving instructions in the Will probably won't work.

A good way to provide funeral or burial instructions is in a separate document called a Designation of Intention or Designation of Agent for Disposition of Remains form. This document should be left in a place that is accessible. If you place this document in a safe deposit box, it may not be available in time for those planning your funeral to follow your instructions. Safe deposit boxes can be sealed when a bank receives notice of one's death. So this is one document that you should leave in a location in your home where it is easy to locate. And make sure that others know about it. You could also give it to your executor or the person who will be responsible for your burial.

It is particularly important to have such a document if you've already purchased a funeral plot, preplanned your funeral, or have special instructions such as cremation. If that fact doesn't become known until after you've been buried someplace other than where you've directed, then you could end up having two plots, one of which you'll never use. Also, if you've worked with a funeral home to make preparations, you can leave the Designation of Intentions document with them and all your family needs to know is which funeral home to contact.

The need to designate who has the final say can be particularly important when families have divided as a result of a divorce, a prior death, or some other family disruption. This became a serious issue in New York State. The legislature amended the Department of Health law to fix a disturbing recurring problem of family disputes over who was entitled to claim the final remains of deceased soldiers killed in the Middle East conflict. Divorced parents of a returning soldier tried to claim their child's body for burial. Each parent, as the closest next of kin, had equal right to handle the disposition of his remains, but they couldn't agree on a plan and some arguments continued as their son's body remained unclaimed, locked in a divorce stalemate. This disturbing situation led another state to institute a designation form under state law allowing one to designate an agent for future burial who may not be the traditional next of kin. Often legal clients name their executor in this role or name the same person appointed under a Power of Attorney in order to keep things uniform.

There's a good chance you've already been involved with a funeral or two, such as those of your grandparents or parents, so that you have a sense of all the decisions that have to be made. These include whether or not you want to be buried or cremated, the type of casket or urn to be purchased, whether the casket should be open or closed if there is a wake, whether or not you want flowers or would prefer gifts be made to a charity, and so on. Some people say they don't care what happens, and that's fine. In that case, you don't need to leave any specific directions. But even people who don't really care all that much do leave some directions so that their family isn't left with the difficult job of making those choices, especially if there are differing opinions. One reason for doing the planning in advance is that, as we've already discussed, sometimes families start squabbling over even simple burial matters. If you feel that your family may be of that type, you'll want to do what you can to prevent that from occurring. When emotions are high as they are after the death of a loved one, rational behavior can sometimes be pushed aside by irrational emotions, so it's best to make all the decisions yourself and write them down.

Another reason for making your intentions known is to communicate from the grave, so to speak. Clark Gable left instructions that he wanted to be buried next to his former wife, not his most recent wife, telling the world where his heart truly resided.

Whether or not your family is bound to follow your wishes, there's a good chance that they will if you've gone to the trouble of setting those wishes down on paper. Depending on what you wish to do and the state you live in, your lawyer can advise you how to best go about making sure your wishes are honored regarding the manner in which you are laid to rest.

There's another reason to make plans ahead of time for when you die. Those closest to you who will be making the arrangements are likely to be very emotional. Unscrupulous funeral directors may take advantage of this emotional state and pressure them to buy the most expensive casket. You can, of course, consult with your family members when making your plans, but by planning ahead you can make the process of being laid to rest a lot easier and less stressful.

Prepaying your funeral expenses, or preplanning your funeral, may be financially beneficial. Medicaid rules do not count funds spent on a prepaid funeral in determining asset eligibility levels. Since funeral expenses can be significant, this is a good way to set aside funds that won't count when calculating when Medicaid will begin paying for expenses such as nursing home care. Each state has different laws on how this can be done, so it's a topic that you should discuss with your elder law attorney.

~

CHAPTER SIX

Digital Estate Planning: The Digital Diary

It's becoming more important to put an end to your life in cyberspace after you die, and this document will help those left behind handle this task.

The final document in the 5@55 suite is of fairly recent origin and has to do with your electronic identities. It is a new addition to the menu of legal planning documents that addresses the needs of the millions of us who use computers to transact business, for social interactions, and for everyday communications. These days you probably are registered in some way on dozens of websites, including social media outlets like Facebook, Twitter, and Instagram. Do you want your presence to continue on these sites after your death? Probably not (though some people, up to 30 percent, do). But unless someone actively closes these accounts, they'll be up there forever since most of them don't require the payment of any fees that would automatically cause them to lapse after nonpayment. You probably also have a presence on websites where you shop, such as Amazon or eBay. And if you shop on the web, you may have an account with PayPal. If you travel, you may have frequent-flier-mile accounts on one or more airline websites. If you do your banking or investments online, your information is on those sites as well. Lastly, many people store all sorts of data in the "cloud," including photos, music files, and potentially important and private documents.

Identity thieves don't really care whether you are dead or alive, but it probably does make it a bit easier for them if you, their victim, has passed away because you wouldn't be able to catch them at their nefarious deeds. While you are alive and able to check, you may notice that your computer/tablet/mobile phone has been hacked and your identity stolen. Once you're not around, thieves might be able to pose as you for a long time. In fact, one man was arrested for having filed false tax returns for many dead people, resulting in his receiving nonexistent tax refunds, by using information he found on the web. So your best bet is to make sure that after you've left this real world, you've also left the virtual electronic one.

In order to close all these accounts, your executor, or a designated agent, is going to need a list of all your identities and passwords. If this list is printed out and kept somewhere, they'd have to know where to find it. Of course if you print out the list and keep it next to your computer, which some experts recommend, even the best hackers can't get at it. However, such a list would be vulnerable either to a thief who breaks in and takes the computer or to snooping family members. To prevent those possible intrusions, you could code your written list using a key that you hide elsewhere (as long as your executor or agent knows where to find it).

If you keep a list of passwords and other information required by website registrations (such as the answers to questions like your mother's maiden name) on your computer, and it's up to date, then making sure that this list gets into the right hands should be easy. If you use a password to lock your computer, then that may be the most important password to pass on. You may also keep lots of other financial records on your home computer, especially if you do your taxes on it. Those records could be very useful to your executor, but he or she would need access. The following case shows what can happen when you do not make plans to pass on your access codes and passwords:

Jim was an avid user of his computer. As a double amputee with limited mobility, he relied on his computer to order most everything he needed. He paid his bills online, and his accounts were listed ready for use. He kept an inventory of his extensive and valuable vinyl record and book collections. He listed all his friends and contacts on the computer, his doctors, the handyman, and the plumber, and cataloged all the repairs he made and the expenses he incurred on his meticulously renovated brownstone.

These records were very helpful to his accountant in doing his annual taxes and calculating future capital gains taxes. Jim prided himself on his order and completeness and often told his family and friends he could get at any information with ease—it was only a click away. The only tragedy was when Jim became ill, his appointed agent under a POA was unable to access the computer. Jim, being extremely conscientious, had changed his passwords frequently and failed to update his agent on the new passwords. When he died, his preciously cataloged information was sealed as securely as his coffin. It took several weeks of computer hacking (and a great deal of geek dollars) to unlock his computer's secrets.

Unfortunately for Jim, all his rather private and personal viewing materials were also unlocked, much to his family's dismay. The moral of the story is that you should encrypt materials you want to be private, but make sure that the information the agent you appoint in your POA, your executor, or your trustee needs to handle your affairs is fully accessible. If you change your passwords frequently, as we are encouraged to do, then make sure you keep a record available for the agent to stay up to date. Reliance on digital memory was a wonderful aid to Jim in life, but he did not provide access to his computer log-in information and passwords to those assigned to help him. Thus, his paperless system was an unfortunate roadblock that added to the costs of helping him and later settling his estate.

These days so many different types of information can be stored on computers or up in the electronic cloud. If you have files that you don't want anyone else to see then you have to let your executor know which files need to be deleted before anyone else can gain access. (And if you were good about backing up your files, then any files you want to be destroyed will also have to be destroyed in any and all places where you backed them up.)

Locating all the files you want deleted could be a major job. One way of making this process less onerous would be to store any files that you definitely want destroyed on your passing only on a separate hard drive rather than on your computer's hard drive with all your other records. Then all your executor would have to do is destroy that one separate drive, which could be done physically—that is, by smashing it rather than connecting it to a computer and deleting everything. Of course every time you wanted to access those files you'd need to plug in that extra drive into your computer, so creating this separate drive would make your life more complicated. It might be something you'd do only if you were in ill health and thought the time had come to protect your privacy in this manner. (Of course bear in mind that even those in the best of health sometimes die in accidents.)

Companies such as PasswordBox and Dashlane say that they can assist in closing your digital life for your family. But since you're not planning on going anytime soon, it's difficult to put your trust in a website that might depart long before you do. (And by the way, did you know that 30 million Facebook users passed away during the first eight years of Facebook's existence?) The better approach is to have the proper documents prepared so that your executor or other family member can settle your e-affairs.

And keep in mind that you don't necessarily have to leave all these chores to your executor. Certainly anything having to do with your finances should be done by your executor, but you could designate someone else, such as a younger family member who may be more computer savvy, to take care of your social networking sites or your photos or music collection stored in the cloud.

HOW A LAWYER CAN HELP

As with the other documents discussed in this book, state laws differ, so you will need to confer with a lawyer in the state in which you reside in order to make sure that any paperwork appointing an agent to handle your cyberspace accounts complies with the law in your state. Delaware is the first state whose legislature has passed a law allowing families access rights to their dearly departed's web presence, and other states are considering similar laws. It's expected that most states will soon have them, and there is a national conference now working on a model law that each of the states can model or adopt.

The first step in the process of digital estate planning is to make what we call a Digital Diary. This is a list of your entire online presence with passwords and other information necessary to access all the sites next to the name. If when preparing this list you note that you've used the same password for many of these sites, this would be a good time to increase your online security by changing these passwords. Make sure all passwords, new or old, are long enough to prevent hackers from easily guessing them.

Your Digital Diary should include the passwords to any electronic devices you own, including your desktop computer, laptop, tablet, and smartphone; your Internet service provider; your email accounts; social networking sites such as Facebook, Twitter, Flickr, and LinkedIn; financial sites such as banks, PayPal, brokerage firms, college savings plans, and retirement accounts; any company or agency where you have set up an automatic payment plan such as EZPass; online subscriptions; retail companies such as Amazon or iTunes; and software companies such as those that protect your computer from viruses and malware. (You can find a sample list in Appendix E: The Digital Diary. Since there are so many possible websites where you might have a password, we haven't tried to list all of them, but rather list several as examples.)

Once you've listed everything and decided whom you will entrust with access to all assets in your digital estate, you then want to leave your executor, representative, or agent(s) instructions on what you want done. Do you want to close everything, set up memorials, or leave others in charge? In some instances, the law will have to be followed and your lawyer can guide you. And if you were thinking about putting any user names and passwords in your Will, your lawyer will stop you because a Will becomes a public document once it is filed with the court.

As of this writing, many of the more popular social media sites are trying to figure out what to do when members pass on. For now there are ways to delete yourself, but they may not be complete. If your heirs can't delete your presence on sites such as Facebook, they should at least be able to change your privacy settings, limiting how much information about you people can access. Then, even if "you" can't be erased from a website, the information about you is somewhat protected.

There is a website called **justdelete.me** that lists many of the possible web accounts you might have, rates how easy or hard they are to delete your name from, and provides instructions about how to do this. This is a good website to look at if for no other reason than it gives you a pretty comprehensive list of potential sites you may have to consider being deleted from.

By the way, there is one site that may always be impossible to wipe clean—the Internet Archive. The aim of this website is to catalog everything on the web and create a giant digital library. Since its purpose is to keep everything on the web available forever, it won't easily erase anything. So perhaps the most important thing to know about this site is simply that it exists, and that you should never post online anything that you would not want to share with your family, friends, and others for posterity.

Conclusion

So many of today's most popular TV shows feature ordinary folk trying to overcome a series of challenges thought up by the producers. It's called "reality" television, but let's face it, in reality you're never going to find yourself on a desert island struggling to get through an obstacle course. Such shows might be entertaining, but they don't depict anything resembling real life. Fate, on the other hand, can place you in situations that are far more challenging than those found on a TV show. But if you've planned ahead, the blow to you and your family can be softened. Perhaps you know the feeling of security that having health, fire, accident, or life insurance can bring. Having the 5@55 documents can instill in you similar feelings of security from a number of dangers that are all too real.

In this book, we've show you examples of the challenges you could face in your own life. As you've seen, a failure to plan ahead can lead to severe consequences. But you can take charge *right now*. You can shout "Action" and then leap over tall buildings in a single bound . . . or at least step into the offices of a lawyer.

The stories we've included in this book weren't created by TV writers. Not only is every one of them true, but they each represent hundreds more. We've only shown you the tip of the iceberg. However, the purpose of this book isn't to entertain you by offering a peep hole into the troubled lives of others, but rather to make sure that you, our reader, doesn't fall victim to a similar fate. We want you to take this information and use it to motivate yourself to obtain the protection and peace of mind that the 5@55 documents offer you and your family.

Here are the steps you should take to save yourself from becoming the star of your own reality horror show:

1. Fill in the questionnaire in Appendix A: Client Questionnaire. Pulling together all this information will help you make the right decisions.
2. If you're married, have a conversation with your spouse about the issues discussed in this book.
3. If you don't already have an attorney, ask people you know and trust for references. Or consult the list of attorneys in Appendix H: The 5@55 Campaign.
4. Make an appointment for a consultation with a lawyer experienced in preparing the 5@55 documents.
5. Carefully consider the options you are offered.
6. Tell your lawyer what you want to do and *follow through* with the process.

We've emphasized the words "follow through" because over and over again we attorneys have people come in to see us, only to then they drop the ball. Sometimes this happens even after all the paperwork has been completed and all they need to do to activate this legal coverage is to sign their names on the dotted lines. Why does this occur? Each case is different, but there are some factors shared by many. One is avoidance in making decisions. Your lawyer won't tell you what to do but instead will give you a menu of options. For some people, making those choices is difficult, so rather than face them they sweep them under the rug.

Others don't really want to face up to the future and their own death. They start the process but at some point decide that the exercise is too emotional. Sometimes the hurdle is a dispute between husband and wife, with one wanting one thing and the other the opposite. And, by the way, this disagreement may have little to do with the actual papers but could be something else entirely. Perhaps he wants to retire in Florida and she doesn't, and so every aspect of their future planning gets put in a locked box.

(Lawyers aren't marital counselors, but sometimes going back for a further consultation will help get you through such a logjam.)

Again, we gave you all those examples in the book for a reason: to motivate you into being prepared for the most likely eventualities. If necessary, reread some of these stories. Soak in the fact that life was good for these people, but then, "in a New York minute," something occurred that made life a lot more difficult. Having the proper paperwork in place would have eased their burden considerably.

And what if you already have some or all of these documents but they're quite old? Should you have them redrawn or are they good enough as is? The answer to this question will depend on your situation. Sometimes the answer is obvious, such as when the person you designate as your agent in one of these documents is no longer available or suitable.

Review your documents with your lawyer at least every five years to make sure that you stay fully protected.

If important circumstances in your life have changed—perhaps you've divorced and remarried—then the need for new paperwork should be obvious. But even if everything in your life has remained the same, the laws themselves may have changed. These changes can affect things like your spouse's rights and estate taxes, and could make earlier good decisions less than optimal. That doesn't mean that your documents are no longer valid, but it could mean that they could be improved. Lawyers must take courses in their field every year, so your attorney will know what if any changes you might need. We suggest a consultation with your lawyer at least every five years to review your documents in order to make sure that you're fully protected.

And remember that you're taking these steps not so much for yourself but for your family members. When these papers kick in, it means that you aren't fit to take action yourself. So for the sake of your loved ones, as well as the security of knowing that your wishes will be honored, do what needs to be done before it's too late.

Weather forecasters would love to give you forecasts of only sunny days but alas they cannot. All they can do is tell you it's going to rain so you can grab an umbrella before you go out. We wish we could offer you a future free of troubles, but that's beyond our abilities. What we can offer you is the 5@55 shield to deflect the full effect of the storms you may have to weather. Just remember that those 5@55 documents, like that umbrella, can do no good if they're left in the hall closet.

Appendices

A NOTE ABOUT THE 5@55 DOCUMENTS THAT FOLLOW

The sample Health Care Proxy, Power of Attorney, and Living Will that follow are examples of documents described in this book. These sample documents may not comply with the laws of the state in which you reside. These documents and other legal documents referenced in this book should be executed under the supervision of a qualified attorney licensed to practice law in your state.

APPENDIX A: CLIENT QUESTIONNAIRE

This is the questionnaire that we use at our law firm. We ask new clients to fill this out before meeting with an attorney in order to save time. Each law firm processes new clients differently, but this form will provide you with the type of information that every law firm needs to prepare your paperwork.

TYPE OF CASE

_____ Estate Planning   Staff Assigned _____

_____ Estate Administration   Client # Assigned _____

                                Client Code _____

CLIENT INFORMATION (PERSON[S] RECEIVING THE BILL)

Name _____

Address _____

City _____ State _____ Zip _____

Phone Home _____ Work _____

Cell _____ Fax _____

Email _____

Relationship to Person in Need _____

Referred by: Name _____

Address _____

PERSON WHO NEEDS ASSISTANCE (IF NOT CLIENT)

Name _____

Address _____

City _____ State _____ Zip _____

Phone Home _____ Work _____

Cell _____ Fax _____

Email _____

Birth Date _____

Retirement Date _____

Occupation _____

Social Security Number _____

Union: ☐ Yes ☐ No   Veteran: ☐ Yes ☐ No

OTHER CONTACT PERSON

Name _____

Address _____

City _____ State _____ Zip_____

Phone Home_____ Work _____

Cell _____ Fax _____

Email _____

Relationship to Person in Need _____

SPOUSE/DOMESTIC PARTNER

Married: ☐ Yes ☐ No

Name _____

Birth Date _____

Retirement Date _____

Occupation _____

Social Security Number _____

Union: ☐ Yes ☐ No   Veteran: ☐ Yes ☐ No

FAMILY DESCRIPTION

Number of Children_____ Names _____

Number of Grandchildren _____

Special Comments/Notes_____

_____

REAL PROPERTY INFORMATION

Primary Residence: ☐ Single Family   ☐ Multiple Family   ☐ Co-op
                     ☐ Condominium   ☐ Other _____

Mortgage Payment _____ Market Value_____

Purchase Price _____ Purchase Date _____

☐ Rent: Monthly Rent_____

Secondary Residence: ☐ Single Family   ☐ Multiple Family   ☐ Co-op
                     ☐ Condominium   ☐ Other _____

Mortgage Payment _____ Market Value_____

Purchase Price _____ Purchase Date _____

INCOME

	Person in Need	Spouse	Comments
Social Security			
Pension			
Other			
Health Insurance			
Monthly Premium			

INSURANCE

Life Insurance:

Company	Policy Number	Face Value	Cash Value	Owner	Beneficiary

Medicare Card: ☐ Yes ☐ No

Primary Health Insurance:

	Person in Need	Spouse
Company		
Policy Number		
Premium Amount		
HMO		
Standard		

Additional Health Insurance:

	Person in Need	Spouse
Company		
Policy Number		
Premium Amount		
HMO		
Standard		

Long-Term Care Insurance:

	Person in Need	Spouse
Company		
Policy Number		
Coverage		

MEDICAL INFORMATION

Primary Care Physician:

Name _____   Phone _____

Address _____

_____

Health Care Needs That Require Special Attention_____

_____

_____

FINANCIAL INFORMATION

Financial Advisor/Broker:

Name _____   Phone _____

Address _____

_____

Accountant/Tax Preparer:

Name _____   Phone _____

Address _____

_____

Bank Accounts:

Bank	Type of Account	Account Name	Account Number	Amount	Dates

Stocks/ Investment Accounts:

Company	Number of Shares	Account Name	Account Number	Present Value	Date of Purchase

Bonds/ Funds:

Company	Maturation Date	Account Name	Account Number	Present Value	Date of Purchase

Retirement Accounts, IRAs, Annuities, T-Bills, or Other Accounts:

Company	Account Number	Face Value	Cash Value	Owner	Beneficiary

APPENDIX B: HEALTH CARE PROXY

(1) I, _____, residing at_____

Hereby appoint _____, residing at_____

Tel: _____

(name, home address, and telephone number)

as my health care agent to make any and all health care decisions for me, except to the extent that I state otherwise. This proxy shall take effect when and if I become unable to make my own health care decisions.

(2) Optional Instructions: I direct my proxy to make health care decisions in accord with my wishes and limitations as stated below, or as he or she otherwise knows. (Attach additional pages if necessary.)

<u>My agent and my substitute agent are aware of my wishes regarding artificial nutrition and hydration, and I authorize my agent and my substitute agent to make decisions in that regard.</u>

(Unless your agent knows your wishes about artificial nutrition and hydration feeding tubes, your agent will not be allowed to make decisions about artificial nutrition and hydration. See the preceding instructions for samples of language you could use.)

(3) Name of substitute or fill-in proxy if the person I appoint above is unable, unwilling, or unavailable to act as my health care agent.

_____

Or, if he/she is unable, unwilling or unavailable to act as my health care agent, I appoint

_____

Or, if he/she is unable, unwilling, or unavailable to act as my health care agent, I appoint

_____

(4) In addition to other powers granted by me in this document, my agent shall have the power and authority to serve as my personal representative for all purposes of the Health Insurance Portability and Accountability Act. My agent is authorized to execute any and all

releases and other documents necessary in order to obtain disclosure of my patient records and other medical information subject to and protected under HIPAA.

(5) Optional: Organ and/or Tissue Donation

I hereby make an anatomical gift, to be effective upon my death, of: (check any that apply)

☐ Any needed organs and/or tissues

☐ The following organs and/or tissues _____

☐ Limitations _____

If you do not state your wishes or instructions about organ and/or tissue donation on this form, it will not be taken to mean that you do not wish to make a donation or prevent a person, who is otherwise authorized by law, to consent to a donation on your behalf.

(6) Unless I revoke it, this Proxy shall remain in effect indefinitely, or until the date or condition stated below. This proxy shall expire (specific date or conditions, if desired):

(7) Signature _____

Address _____

Date _____

Statement by Witnesses (Must be 18 or older)

I declare that the person who signed this document is personally known to me and appears to be of sound mind and acting of his or her own free will. He or she signed (or asked another to sign for him or her) this document in my presence.

Witness 1 _____

Address _____

Witness 2 _____

Address _____

POWER OF ATTORNEY
NEW YORK STATUTORY SHORT FORM

(a) CAUTION TO THE PRINCIPAL: Your Power of Attorney is an important document. As the "principal," you give the person whom you choose (your "agent") authority to spend your money and sell or dispose of your property during your lifetime without telling you. You do not lose your authority to act even though you have given your agent similar authority.

When your agent exercises this authority, he or she must act according to any instructions you have provided or, where there are no specific instructions, in your best interest. "Important Information for the Agent" at the end of this document describes your agent's responsibilities.

Your agent can act on your behalf only after signing the Power of Attorney before a notary public.

You can request information from your agent at any time. If you are revoking a prior Power of Attorney, you should provide written notice of revocation to your prior agent(s) and to any third parties who may have acted upon it, including the financial institutions where your accounts are located.

You can revoke or terminate your Power of Attorney at any time for any reason as long as you are of sound mind. If you are no longer of sound mind, a court can remove an agent for acting improperly.

Your agent cannot make health care decisions for you. You may execute a "Health Care Proxy" to do this.

The law governing Powers of Attorney is contained in the New York General Obligations Law, Article 5, Title 15. This law is available at a law library, or online through the New York State Senate or Assembly websites, www.senate.state.ny.us or www.assembly.state.ny.us.

If there is anything about this document that you do not understand, you should ask a lawyer of your own choosing to explain it to you.

This document is authorized for use in New York State by a New York State resident. It may not be legally enforceable in any other state. The form of this document used in the state in which you reside should only be executed under the supervision of a qualified attorney licensed to practice law in your state.

(b) DESIGNATION OF AGENT(S):

I, _____, residing at _____

hereby appoint:

_____, residing at _____

as my agent(s)

If you designate more than one agent above, they must act together unless you initial the statement below.

[_____] My agents may act SEPARATELY.

(c) DESIGNATION OF SUCCESSOR AGENT(S): (OPTIONAL)

If any agent designated above is unable or unwilling to serve, I appoint as my successor agent(s):

Successor agents designated above must act together unless you initial the statement below.

[_____] My successor agents may act SEPARATELY.

You may provide for specific succession rules in this section. Insert specific succession provisions here:

(d) This POWER OF ATTORNEY shall not be affected by my subsequent incapacity unless I have stated otherwise below, under "Modifications."

(e) This POWER OF ATTORNEY DOES NOT REVOKE any Powers of Attorney previously executed by me unless I have stated otherwise below, under "Modifications."

If you do NOT intend to revoke your prior Powers of Attorney, and if you have granted the same authority in this Power of Attorney as you granted to another agent in a prior Power of Attorney, each agent can act separately unless you indicated under "Modifications" that the agents with the same authority are to act together.

(f) GRANT OF AUTHORITY: To grant your agent some or all of the authority below, either

(1) Initial the bracket at each authority you grant, or

(2) Write or type the letters for each authority you grant on the blank line at (P), and initial the bracket at (P). If you initial (P), you do not need to initial the other lines.

I grant authority to my agent(s) with respect to the following subjects as defined in sections 5-1502A through 5-1502N of the New York General Obligations Law:

[_____] (A) real estate transactions;

[_____] (B) chattel and goods transactions;

[_____] (C) bond, share, and commodity transactions;

[_____] (D) banking transactions;

[_____] (E) business operating transactions;

[_____] (F) insurance transactions;

[_____] (G) estate transactions;

[_____] (H) claims and litigation;

[_____] (I) personal and family maintenance: If you grant your agent this authority, it will allow the agent to make gifts that you customarily have made to individuals, including the agent, and charitable organizations. The total amount of all such gifts in any one calendar year cannot exceed five hundred dollars;

[_____] (J) benefits from governmental programs or civil or military service;

[_____] (K) health care billing and payment matters; records, reports, and statements; **you need not initial the other lines if you initial line (P).**

[_____] (L) retirement benefit transactions;

[_____] (M) tax matters;

[_____] (N) all other matters;

[_____] (O) full and unqualified authority to my agent(s) to delegate any or all of the foregoing powers to any person or persons whom my agent(s) select;

[_____] (P) EACH of the matters identified by the following letters <u>A</u> through <u>O</u>.

(g) MODIFICATIONS: (OPTIONAL)

In this section, you may make additional provisions, including language to limit or supplement authority granted to your agent. However, you cannot use this Modifications section to grant your agent authority to make gifts or changes to interests in your property. If you wish to grant your agent such authority, you MUST complete the Statutory Gifts Rider.

[_____] This Power of Attorney revokes any prior Powers of Attorney as noted: _____

_____

[_____] This Power of Attorney provides that the agent can participate in medical, estate, and tax planning including representing the Principal in the matter concerning Medicare, Medicaid, Social Security, and other government programs.

[_____] To sell or purchase a life estate on behalf of the Principal.

[_____] To make decisions regarding my domicile or residence including executing documents and issuing statements concerning my intentions with respect to my residency or domicile, or relinquishing or revoking my right to occupy any residence.

[_____] I wish to set a compensation schedule for my agent(s) as follows:

_____

_____

[_____] Unless reasonable cause exists to require otherwise, the agent(s) shall not be obligated by the monitor to provide financial details or accountings more frequently than annually.

(h) CERTAIN GIFT TRANSACTIONS: STATUTORY GIFTS RIDER (OPTIONAL)

In order to authorize your agent to make gifts in excess of an annual total of $500 for all gifts described in (I) of the grant of authority section of this document (under personal and family maintenance), you must initial the statement below and execute a Statutory Gifts Rider at the same time as this instrument. Initialing the statement below by itself does not authorize your agent to make gifts. The preparation of the Statutory Gifts Rider should be **supervised by a lawyer.**

[_____] (SGR) I grant my agent authority to make gifts in accordance with the terms and conditions of the Statutory Gifts Rider that supplements this Statutory Power of Attorney.

This document is authorized for use in New York State by a New York State resident. It may not be legally enforceable in any other state. The form of this document used in the state in which you reside should only be executed under the supervision of a qualified attorney licensed to practice law in your state.

(i) DESIGNATION OF MONITOR(S): (OPTIONAL)

If you wish to appoint monitor(s), initial and fill in the section below:

[_____] I wish to designate   [_____] I do not wish to designate a
monitor

_____ whose address is _____

_____ whose address is _____

as monitor(s). Upon the request of the monitor(s), my agent(s) must provide the monitor(s) with a copy of the power of attorney and a record of all transactions done or made on my behalf. Third parties holding records of such transactions shall provide the records to the monitor(s) upon request.

(j) COMPENSATION OF AGENT(S): (OPTIONAL)

Your agent is entitled to be reimbursed from your assets for reasonable expenses incurred on your behalf. If you ALSO wish your agent(s) to be compensated from your assets for services rendered on your behalf, initial the statement below. If you wish to define "reasonable compensation," you may do so above, under "Modifications."

[_____] My agent(s) shall be entitled to reasonable compensation for services rendered.

(k) ACCEPTANCE BY THIRD PARTIES:

I agree to indemnify the third party for any claims that may arise against the third party because of reliance on this Power of Attorney. I understand that any termination of this Power of Attorney, whether the result of my revocation of the Power of Attorney or otherwise, is not effective as to a third party until the third party has actual notice or knowledge of the termination.

(l) TERMINATION:

This Power of Attorney continues until I revoke it or it is terminated by my death or other event described in section 5-1511 of the General Obligations Law.

Section 5-1511 of the General Obligations Law describes the manner in which you may revoke your Power of Attorney, and the events which terminate the Power of Attorney.

(m) SIGNATURE AND ACKNOWLEDGMENT:

In Witness Whereof I have hereunto signed my name on _____, 2015.

PRINCIPAL signs here: ➡ _____

ACKNOWLEDGEMENT IN NEW YORK STATE (RPL 309-a)

State of

County of   ss.

On   before me, the undersigned, personally appeared personally known to me or proved to me on the basis of satisfactory evidence to be the individual whose name is subscribed to the within instrument and acknowledged to me he/she executed the same in his/her capacity, and that by his/her capacity, and that by his/her signature on the instrument, the individual, or the person on behalf of which the individual acted, executed the instrument.

_____
(signature and office of individual taking acknowledgement)

ACKNOWLEDGEMENT OUTSIDE NEW YORK STATE (RPL 309-b)

State of

County of   ss.

On   before me, the undersigned, personally appeared personally known to me or proved to me on the basis of satisfactory evidence to be the individual whose name is subscribed to the within instrument and acknowledged to me that he/she executed the same in his/her capacity, and that by his/her signature on the instrument, the individual, or the person upon behalf of which the individual acted, executed the instrument, and that such individual made such appearance before the undersigned in

(insert city or political subdivision and state or country or other place acknowledgement taken)

_____
(signature and office of individual taking acknowledgement)

(n) IMPORTANT INFORMATION FOR THE AGENT:

When you accept the authority granted under this Power of Attorney, a special legal relationship is created between you and the principal. This relationship imposes on you legal responsibilities that continue until you resign or the Power of Attorney is terminated or revoked. You must:

(1) act according to any instructions from the principal, or, where there are no instructions, in the principal's best interest;

(2) avoid conflicts that would impair your ability to act in the principal's best interest;

(3) keep the principal's property separate and distinct from any assets you own or control, unless otherwise permitted by law;

(4) keep a record or all receipts, payments, and transactions conducted for the principal; and

(5) disclose your identity as an agent whenever you act for the principal by writing or printing the principal's name and signing your own name as "agent" in either of the following manner: (Principal's Name) by (Your Signature) as Agent, or (Your Signature) as Agent for (Principal's Name).

You may not use the principal's assets to benefit yourself or anyone else or make gifts to yourself or anyone else unless the principal has specifically granted you that authority in this document, which is either a Statutory Gifts Rider attached to a Statutory Short Form Power of Attorney or a Non-Statutory Power of Attorney. If you have that authority, you must act according to any instructions of the principal or, where there are no such instructions, in the principal's best interest.

You may resign by giving written notice to the principal and to any co-agent, successor agent, or monitor if one has been named in this document, or the principal's guardian if one has been appointed. If there is anything about this document or your responsibilities that you do not understand, you should seek legal advice.

Liability of agent: The meaning of the authority given to you is defined in New York's General Obligations Law, Article 5, Title 15. If it is found that you have violated the law or acted outside the authority granted to you in the Power of Attorney, you may be liable under the law for your violation.

(o) AGENT'S SIGNATURE AND ACKNOWLEDGMENT OF APPOINTMENT:

It is not required that the principal and the agent(s) sign at the same time, nor that multiple agents sign at the same time.

I/we, _____, have read the foregoing Power of Attorney. I am/we are the person(s) identified therein as agent(s) for the principal named therein.

I/we acknowledge my/our legal responsibilities.

Agent(s) sign(s) here: ➡ _____

ACKNOWLEDGEMENT IN NEW YORK STATE (RPL 309-a)

State of
County of   ss.

On   before me, the undersigned, personally appeared personally known to me or proved to me on the basis of satisfactory evidence to be the individual(s) whose name(s) is (are) subscribed to the within instrument and acknowledged to me he/she/they executed the same in his/her/their capacity(ies), and that by his/her/their capacity(ies), and that by his/her/their signature(s) on the instrument, the individual(s), or the person on behalf of which the individual(s) acted, executed the instrument.

_____
(signature and office of individual taking acknowledgement)

ACKNOWLEDGEMENT OUTSIDE NEW YORK STATE (RPL 309-b)

State of
County of   ss.

On   before me, the undersigned, personally appeared personally known to me or proved to me on the basis of satisfactory evidence to be the individual(s) whose name(s) is (are) subscribed to the within instrument and acknowledged to me that he/she/they executed the same in his/her/their capacity(ies), and that by his/her/their signature(s) on the instrument, the individual(s), or the person upon behalf of which the individual(s) acted, executed the instrument, and that such individual made such appearance before the undersigned in

_____
(insert city or political subdivision and state or country or other place acknowledgement taken)

_____
(signature and office of individual taking acknowledgement)

(p) SUCCESSOR AGENT'S SIGNATURE AND ACKNOWLEDGEMENT OF APPOINTMENT:

It is not required that the principal and the SUCCESSOR agent(s), if any, sign at the same time, nor that multiple SUCCESSOR agents sign at the same time. Furthermore, successor agents cannot use this Power of Attorney unless the agent(s) designated above is/are unable or unwilling to serve.

I/we, _____ have read the foregoing Power of Attorney. I am/we are the person(s) identified therein as SUCCESSOR agent(s) for the principal named therein.

Successor Agent(s) sign(s) here: ➡ _____

ACKNOWLEDGEMENT IN NEW YORK STATE (RPL 309-a)

State of
County of   ss.

On   before me, the undersigned, personally appeared personally known to me or proved to me on the basis of satisfactory evidence to be the individual(s) whose name(s) is (are) subscribed to the within instrument and acknowledged to me he/she/they executed the same in his/her/their capacity(ies), and that by his/her/their capacity(ies), and that by his/her/their signature(s) on the instrument, the individual(s), or the person on behalf of which the individual(s) acted, executed the instrument.

_____
(signature and office of individual taking acknowledgement)

ACKNOWLEDGEMENT OUTSIDE NEW YORK STATE (RPL 309-b)

State of
County of   ss.

On   before me, the undersigned, personally appeared personally known to me or proved to me on the basis of satisfactory evidence to be the individual(s) whose name(s) is (are) subscribed to the within instrument and acknowledged to me that he/she/they executed the same in his/her/their capacity(ies), and that by his/her/their signature(s) on the instrument, the individual(s), or the person upon behalf of which the individual(s) acted, executed the instrument, and that such individual made such appearance before the undersigned in

(insert city or political subdivision and state or country or other place acknowledgement taken)

_____
(signature and office of individual taking acknowledgement)

POWER OF ATTORNEY
NEW YORK STATUTORY GIFTS RIDER

AUTHORIZATION TO MAKE CERTAIN GIFT TRANSACTIONS

CAUTION TO THE PRINCIPAL: This OPTIONAL rider allows you to authorize your agent to make gifts in excess of an annual amount total of $500 for all gifts described in (I) of the Grant of Authority section of the statutory short form Power of Attorney (under personal and family maintenance), or certain other gift transactions during your lifetime. You do not have to execute this rider if you only want your agent to make gifts described in (I) of the Grant of Authority section of the statutory short form Power of Attorney and you initialed "(I)" on that section of that form. Granting any of the following authority to your agent gives your agent the authority to take actions which could significantly reduce your property or change how your property is distributed at your death. "Certain gift transactions" are described in section 5-1514 of the General Obligations Law. This Gifts Rider does not require your agent to exercise granted authority, but when he or she exercises this authority, he or she must act according to any instructions you provide, or otherwise in your best interest.

This Gifts Rider and the Power of Attorney it supplements must be read together as a single instrument.

Before signing this document authorizing your agent to make gifts, you should seek legal advice to ensure that your intentions are clearly and properly expressed.

(a) GRANT OF LIMITED AUTHORITY TO MAKE GIFTS

Granting gifting authority to your agent gives your agent the authority to take actions which could significantly reduce your property.

If you wish to allow your agent to make gifts to himself or herself, you must separately grant that authority in subdivision (c) below.

To grant your agent the gifting authority provided below, initial the bracket to the left of the authority.

[_____] I grant authority to my agent to make gifts to my spouse, children and more remote descendants, and parents, not to exceed, for each donee, the annual federal gift tax exclusion amount pursuant to the Internal Revenue Code. For gifts to my children and more remote descendants, and parents, the maximum amount of the gift to each donee shall not exceed twice the gift tax exclusion amount, if my spouse agrees to split gift treatment pursuant to the Internal Revenue Code. This authority must be exercised pursuant to my instructions, or otherwise for purposes which the agent reasonably deems to be in my best interest.

(b) MODIFICATIONS:

Use this section if you wish to authorize gifts in amounts smaller than the gift tax exclusion amount, in amounts in excess of the gift tax exclusion amount, gifts to other beneficiaries, or other gift transactions. Granting such authority to your agent gives your agent the authority to take actions which could significantly reduce your property and/or change how your property is distributed at your death. If you wish to authorize your agent to make gifts to himself or herself, you must separately grant that authority in subdivision (c) below.

[_____] 1. I grant the following authority to my agent to make gifts or transfers pursuant to my instructions, or otherwise for purposes which the agent reasonably deems to be in my best interest.

[_____] 2. The class of beneficiaries for gifting is expanded as follows to include:

_____

_____

[_____] 3. Gifting powers include the following actions and may be in excess of the federal annual gift tax exclusion;

[_____] 3a. To make gifts in amount limited to: _____ (specify amount);

[_____] 3b. To make gifts in unlimited amounts;

[_____] 4. To make the following specified transactions:

a. open, modify or terminate a deposit account, joint account, bank account in trust form, transfer on death account, and any other types of accounts held in any financial institution. "Financial institution" means a financial entity, including, but not limited to: a bank, trust company, national bank, savings bank, federal mutual savings bank, savings and loan association, federal savings and loan association, federal mutual savings and loan association, credit union, branch of a foreign banking corporation, public pension fund, retirement system, securities broker, securities dealer, securities firm, and insurance company, defined by §5-1501 of the New York General Obligations Law.

b. procure new, different or additional life insurance policy or annuity contracts and designate the beneficiary of any such policy or contract to add to or liquidate, in whole or in part, the cash value of any life insurance policy or annuity which I may own as well as to change ownership and beneficiary designations on such policies or contract to any individual, even if such individual is my agent(s).

c. create or contribute to any Individual Retirement Account, pension or employee benefit plan which I may own, have an interest or participate in; to select any payment distribution or option under any Individual Retirement Account, pension or employee benefit plan; and to change any options or beneficiary designations I have selected for such Individual Retirement Account, pension or employee benefit plan, even if such beneficiary is my agent(s).

d.   create, change or terminate other property interests or rights of survivorship, and designate or change the beneficiary or beneficiaries therein.

e.   make transfers and additions to any trusts previously created by me; create trusts on my behalf for Medicaid or estate planning purposes (including trusts created by my agent for benefit of the recipient), to fund such trusts, and to amend, revoke, or terminate *inter vivos* trusts.

f.   execute and deliver a valid disclaimer under the Internal Revenue Code of 1986, as amended, Section 2518 and applicable states' statutes when, in the judgment of my agent(s), the best interests of my estate would be served even if the beneficiary of such disclaimer is my agent(s).

g.   exercise or fail to exercise and thereby release any power of appointment created in my favor under the Internal Revenue Code of 1986, as amended, Section 2041, even if such actions benefit my agent(s).

h.   exercise or deline to exercise or to waive my right of election against my spouse's estate under New York Estate, Powers and Trusts Law, Section 5-1.1A.

i.   authorize to transfer my current residence, or any subsequent residence of any other real property owned by me to any individual or trust even if such individual is my agent(s) or even if my agent(s) is the beneficiary of such trust.

j.   Any gift of my property may be transferred in cash or in kind, and may pass outright to the recipient or may be transferred to a custodian under the Uniform Transfer to Minors Act, or to a tuition savings account or prepaid tuition plan as defined under Section 529 of the Internal Revenue Code.

k.   

[_____] 5. I wish to omit items listed in 4 above identified by_____ from the permissible list of transactions.

(c) GRANT OF SPECIFIC AUTHORITY FOR AN AGENT TO MAKE GIFTS TO HIMSELF OR HERSELF: (OPTIONAL)

If you wish to authorize your agent to make gifts or transfers to himself or herself, you must grant that authority in this section, indicating to which agent(s) the authorization is granted, and any limitations and guidelines.

[_____] I grant specific authority for the following agent(s) to make the gifts to himself or herself, as described above in terms 3 & 4a-k:

My agent(s), _____ and _____may make gifts of my property, in any amount to himself, herself or themselves.

This authority must be exercised pursuant to my instructions, or otherwise for purposes which the agent reasonably deems to be in my best interest.

(d) ACCEPTANCE BY THIRD PARTIES:

I agree to indemnify the third party for any claims that may arise against the third party because of reliance on this Statutory Gifts Rider.

(e) SIGNATURE OF PRINCIPAL AND ACKNOWLEDGMENT:

In Witness Whereof I have hereunto signed my name on _____, 2015.

PRINCIPAL signs here: ➡ _____

ACKNOWLEDGEMENT IN NEW YORK STATE (RPL 309-a)

State of
County of   ss.

On   before me, the undersigned, personally appeared personally known to me or proved to me on the basis of satisfactory evidence to be the individual whose name is subscribed to the within instrument and acknowledged to me he/she executed the same in his/her capacity, and that by his/her capacity, and that by his/her signature on the instrument, the individual, or the person on behalf of which the individual acted, executed the instrument.

_____
(signature and office of individual taking acknowledgement)

ACKNOWLEDGEMENT OUTSIDE NEW YORK STATE (RPL 309-b)

State of
County of   ss.

On   before me, the undersigned, personally appeared personally known to me or proved to me on the basis of satisfactory evidence to be the individual whose name is subscribed to the within instrument and acknowledged to me that he/she executed the same in his/her capacity, and that by his/her signature on the instrument, the individual, or the person upon behalf of which the individual acted, executed the instrument, and that such individual made such appearance before the undersigned in

(insert city or political subdivision and state or country or other place acknowledgement taken)

_____
(signature and office of individual taking acknowledgement)

This document is authorized for use in New York State by a New York State resident. It may not be legally enforceable in any other state. The form of this document used in the state in which you reside should only be executed under the supervision of a qualified attorney licensed to practice law in your state.

(f) SIGNATURES OF WITNESSES:

By signing as a witness, I acknowledge that the principal signed the Statutory Gifts Rider in my presence and the presence of the other witness, or that the principal acknowledged to me that the principal's signature was affixed by him or her or at his or her direction. I also acknowledge that the principal has stated that this Statutory Gifts Rider reflects his or her wishes and that he or she has signed it voluntarily. I am not named herein as a permissible recipient of gifts.

Signature of witness 1	Signature of witness 2
Date	Date
Print name	Print name
Address	Address
City, State, Zip code	City, State, Zip code

(g) This document prepared by:

LIVING WILL

KNOW ALL PEOPLE by these presents that I, _____of the County of _____ State of _____, hereby declare my will with respect to my medical care and treatment in the event I am unable for any reason to make known my will at the time medical decisions must be made.

1. <u>Directive not to use or to discontinue life-prolonging medical treatment when recovery is unlikely.</u>

In the event I suffer from an injury, disease, illness, or other physical or mental condition which renders me unable to make medical decisions on my own behalf, which leaves me unable to communicate with others meaningfully, and from which there is no reasonable prospect of recovery to a cognitive and sentient life, I direct that no medical treatments or procedures be utilized in my care or, if begun, that they be discontinued.

2. <u>Definition of medical treatment.</u>

By "medical treatments or procedures," I mean interventions by medical doctors, nurses, paramedics, or any other health care provider (including a nursing home), in the care of my body and mind, including all medical and surgical procedures, mechanical or otherwise, treatments, therapies, including drugs and hormones, which may substitute for, replace, supplant, enhance, or assist any bodily function. This specifically includes maintenance of respiration, nutrition, and hydration by artificial means. With respect to all medical treatments or procedures, I include

This document is recommended for use in New York State by a New York State resident. It may not be legally enforceable in any other state. The form of this document used in the state in which you reside should only be executed under the supervision of a qualified attorney licensed to practice law in your state.

both existing technology and any methods or techniques which may be hereafter developed and perfected.

3. <u>Provision for pain control</u>.

I ask that medical treatment to alleviate pain, to provide comfort, and to mitigate suffering be provided so that I may be as free of pain and suffering as possible.

4. <u>Determination of prognosis</u>.

My health care agent acting pursuant to my duly executed Health Care Proxy shall follow my directions as set out in this Living Will whenever they have ascertained by reasonable medical standards that my condition is as described in Section 1, above. Absent my health care agent's instructions, any other person shall comply with my directions upon certification that my condition is as described in Section 1, above, by two physicians.

5. <u>Acknowledgment of effects of this Living Will</u>.

I make and execute this Living Will knowing that, if complied with, my death will occur sooner than it would were all available and appropriate medical treatments considered and used. I accept this as a necessary result of a decision to avoid dependence and pain. And I make this decision now, for myself, after careful consideration, to assure that I will have the level of medical care which I want, and to relieve others of the burden of decision.

IN WITNESS WHEREOF, I have hereunto set my hand and seal this _____ day of _____, 2015.

Sign Name: _____

ACKNOWLEDGMENT

_____, the Declarant named in the foregoing instrument, signed this instrument consisting of three (3) typewritten pages (including this attestation page), on the _____ day of _____. At that time, he declared that the instrument reflects his will and intent with respect to his medical care and treatment. At his request, in his presence and in the presence of each other, each of us believing him to be of sound mind, emotionally and mentally competent, we have signed our names as witnesses.

_____ residing at _____

_____ residing at _____

_____ residing at _____

_____

Sample Table of Electronic Information for the Executor

Computer and Other Electronic Equipment

Type	User ID	Password (Indicate if case sensitive)	Name(s) of Files with financial information and/or passwords for executor	Materials to be deleted ASAP: Search History Bookmarks Emails to/from select individuals Files
Desktop				
Laptop/Notebook				
Tablet				
Smartphone				
External storage drive				

Social Media

Name of Website	User ID/Email associated	Password (Indicate if case sensitive)	Answers to Security Question	How to Handle (Close/inactivate, memorialize, set highest privacy level)
Facebook				
Twitter				
LinkedIn				
Pinterest				
Google+				
Other				

Banking and Finance

Name of Institution	User ID/Email associated	Password (Indicate if case sensitive)	Answer(s) to Security Questions	Account number	Type of account (Checking, Savings, Investment, Joint or not)	Paper or paperless
Citibank						
E Trade						
Quicken						
Other						

Cloud Storage

Name of Website	User ID/Email associated	Password (Indicate if case sensitive)	Answer(s) to Security Questions	Type of Information stored
iTunes				Music
Snap Dragon				Photos
Dropbox				Documents
Googledocs				Documents
Gmail				Emails
Other				

Domain Names or Blogs

Name	Host	User ID/Email associated	Password (Indicate if case sensitive)	Answer(s) to Security Question	Type of Account
yourname.com	Namecheap				Website
	Wordpress				Blog

Online Shopping

Name	User ID/Email associated	Password (Indicate if case sensitive)	Account number (if needed)
Amazon			
Macy's			
Zappos			
Others			

Monthly Subscriptions

Name	User ID/Email associated	Password (Indicate if case sensitive)	Answer(s) to security questions	Type of Account
Amazon Subscribe and Save				Shopping
Manpacks				Shopping
The New York Times				Online newspaper
Others				

APPENDIX F: THE ROLE OF AN EXECUTOR

Being selected as an executor is not only an honor but a responsibility to the person who named you, as well as his or her heirs. Acting as executor is a complex job. It requires working with many types of professionals. It is best to rely on a specialized attorney to guide you through the steps in settling the estate, such as an elder law or estate attorney. The executor's role is described below.

Executor's Role
An executor may be an individual, often a family member, or a financial institution, such as a bank or a trust company. A bank or trust company may also serve as a co-executor with an individual who may be the decedent's spouse, child, or any other adult person.

When settling an estate, an executor performs four basic functions:
• Locates and collects assets and is responsible for the estate's assets until they are distributed to the beneficiaries.
• Pays the decedent's funeral expenses, debts, and estate administration expenses.
• Handles tax matters.
  - Files the decedent's final income tax returns and pays the income taxes.
  - Files the estate's income tax returns and pays the estate's income taxes.
  - Files the estate's tax returns and pays the estate taxes, if any.
• Distributes the remaining assets in accordance with the terms of the will.

Considerations
You should consider these qualities when choosing an executor: integrity, knowledge, experience, impartiality, and financial responsibility.

This document is a guide that provides general information about the role of an executor. Requirements of law governing a particular estate and the role of an executor may differ from state to state. Always seek the advice of a licensed, qualified attorney concerning the duties and requirements governing the responsibilities of an executor in your state or in the state governing a particular estate.

Integrity

When you select an executor, a primary consideration should be the integrity of the person. Honesty and the ability to act impartially toward all beneficiaries are essential attributes of an executor.

Knowledge

An executor's initial task is to locate, collect, and, if necessary, take physical possession of assets owned by the decedent. An executor must also protect, insure, and appraise assets, as needed. When necessary, the executor must raise the cash required to pay debts, taxes, and administrative expenses. These financial responsibilities require the executor to make an investment analysis of all assets in the estate and determine which to retain and which to sell, and how the estate's cash needs will be met.

An executor must make sure that no "waste" is committed; otherwise, he/ she may be liable to the beneficiaries for mismanaging the estate assets. All claims against the estate must be carefully evaluated by an executor and either be paid or rejected.

Experience

Much of the administrative work in handling an estate is record keeping and providing close attention to detail. An executor prepares and files the decedent's final federal, state, and local personal income tax returns. For estates with assets exceeding either the federal and/or state estate tax exemption amounts, an executor is responsible for filing a federal estate tax return and, depending upon the jurisdiction, a state estate and/ or inheritance tax return. The federal and state estate tax returns are complex returns *and are due within nine months following the decedent's date of death*. Since the estate is a separate taxpayer, an executor is also required to prepare and file annual income tax returns for the estate.

Impartiality

Depending on the nature and value of the assets, their form of ownership, and the relevant provisions of the Will, the executor will be faced with decisions, referred to as "elections," on the federal estate tax return, which could determine the amount of taxes due. Certain decisions the executor must make, such as tax elections, may have a direct financial impact on each beneficiary. Therefore, a family member or friend must be able to make these decisions impartially. In addition to having the education and training to make these decisions or retain the services of an appropriate professional, an executor must have the objectivity to handle such issues without favoring one beneficiary over another, unless directed to do so under the Will. An executor is advised to secure professional help from an attorney, accountant, or investment advisor in making decisions.

Financial Responsibility

Another major consideration is the accountability and financial responsibility of the individual or entity selected to be the executor. Acting as an executor can be a time-consuming venture lasting several years.

Conclusion

The selection of an executor should not be made solely on the basis of a family relationship or years of friendship. This information should help you to select the best executor for your estate. An experienced estate attorney can work with the appointed executor to achieve an efficient and successful settlement of a decedent's estate.

APPENDIX G: THE TOP TEN DUTIES OF A TRUSTEE

As a trustee, you are considered a "fiduciary," that is, you are responsible for managing the funds and other assets in the Trust and acting in the best interests of all the beneficiaries. The topics below will briefly outline your duties as a trustee.

INCOME: Invest the assets prudently and ensure that the funds generate reasonable income and/or dividends. As a trustee, you are able to use the Trust assets to maintain Trust property, such as real estate, a home, or provide the income to beneficiaries named in the Trust, if the Trust so allows, subject to the terms of the Trust documents.

INVESTMENTS: In deciding on the investments and accounts held by the Trust, you can maintain the grantor's investments (as long as they are reasonably prudent investments) or develop a new investment plan that consolidates the assets and/or creates a more desirable investment return. You should not engage in risky investments unless the Trust specifically allows you to do so. Always consult with an investment advisor to assist you in making these investment choices.

PAYMENTS FROM TRUST HOLDINGS: The Trust principal may be used during the Trust term to maintain or preserve Trust property or as specifically permitted in the Trust documents. You must read all Trust documents carefully and follow the instructions set forth therein.

INCOME TAX: A Trust will be an independent tax payer if an EIN number has been issued for the Trust. As a result, each year the trustee must file a separate income tax return for any income or loss generated by the Trust. You should engage a certified public accountant to file this return. The Trust generally pays income tax at a higher tax rate than an individual. If any income passes to the Grantor or a Trust beneficiary directly, it may be beneficial to pass the corresponding tax liability to these individuals who may have a lower tax rate. Your accountant should review the Trust documents to ascertain the correct party responsible for any or all income taxes due.

This document provides general information about the role of a trustee. Requirements of law governing trusts and the role of a trustee may differ from state to state. Always seek the advice of a licensed, qualified attorney concerning the duties and requirements governing the responsibilities of a trustee in your state or in the state governing a particular Trust.

GIFT TAX: A Trust may or may not be tax neutral or generate a requirement for the filing of a gift tax return, which depends on whether funds placed into the Trust are considered completed gifts. Further, gift tax returns will need to be filed if principal distributions are made to the beneficiaries during the lifetime of the grantor. Your specific Trust will determine the need for filing gift tax returns.

ESTATE TAX: Upon the death of the grantor, the Trust may or may not terminate, depending on the terms of the Trust documents. Do not distribute Trust funds to the beneficiaries until you are certain that there are no estate taxes or other taxes due. If any assets transferred to the Trust are not completed gifts, these assets will be includable in the grantor's estate upon his/her death and the estate may be taxable. These taxes may be due shortly after death.

TRUSTEES: Each Trust names one or more person(s) and/or entity as trustee(s). There may be one primary trustee or primary co-trustees. Depending on the Trust terms, the Trust may have named successor or alternate trustees. Generally, it is advisable for at least one alternative trustee to be named to allow maximum flexibility. Serving as a trustee is voluntary. A trustee's work is completed when the Trust is terminated or when a trustee resigns. Upon resignation, a trustee must account for all Trust activities undertaken during the trustee's term of service.

ACCOUNTINGS AND DUTIES: It is a grantor's duty to identify Trust assets and re-title them into the Trust. Investments should generally follow the relevant state's prudent investor rules. Trust investments should generally be diverse and investments closely monitored. It is important for trustees to retain all the paperwork, statements, etc., to document the expenses and payments made from the Trust fund. Beneficiaries have the right to request an accounting from the trustee. This is especially true if the Trust is subject to a court's jurisdiction or order. An accounting is generally required at the termination of the Trust prior to final distribution to beneficiaries. This accounting covers the whole period during which the trustee acted.

This document provides general information about the role of a trustee. Requirements of law governing trusts and the role of a trustee may differ from state to state. Always seek the advice of a licensed, qualified attorney concerning the duties and requirements governing the responsibilities of a trustee in your state or in the state governing a particular Trust.

<u>COMMISSIONS</u>: As a trustee, you are entitled to commissions which are set by state law based on a percentage of the value of the assets held in a Trust.

<u>SETTLING THE TRUST</u>: A Trust may or may not terminate upon the death of the grantor. When terminated Trust assets must be liquidated or transferred to beneficiaries, accounts must be settled and assets collected and distributed. A trustee usually prepares a simple accounting to be distributed to all beneficiaries with their Trust distribution. Once the accounting is accepted by all beneficiaries, and the relevant court, if required, the Trustee distributes the remainder funds to the beneficiaries named in the Trust.

APPENDIX H: THE 5@55 CAMPAIGN

This book is part of a national educational campaign to build public awareness of the need for the five legal documents described herein by age 55.

FOUNDING MEMBERS

Judith D. Grimaldi, Esq.
Grimaldi & Yeung LLP
9201 4th Avenue, 6th floor
Brooklyn, NY 11209
(718) 238 6960
jgrimaldi@gylawny.com
www.gylawny.com

Joanne Seminara, Esq.
Grimaldi & Yeung LLP
9201 4th Avenue, 6th floor
Brooklyn, NY 11209
(718) 238 6960
jseminara@gylawny.com
www.gylawny.com

CHARTER MEMBERS

Robert C. Anderson, Esq.
Elder Law Firm of Anderson
Associates, PC
148 W Hewitt Avenue
Marquette, MI 49855
(906) 228-6212
rcanderson@upelderlaw.com
www.upelderlaw.com

Jean Galloway Ball, Esq.
Hale Ball Carlson Baumgartner
Murphy, PLC
10306 Eaton Place, Suite 130
Fairfax, VA 22030
(703) 359-9213
jgball@haleball.com
www.haleball.com

Timothy P. Crawford, Esq.
Law Offices of Timothy P.
Crawford, SC
840 Lake Avenue
Racine, WI 53403
(262) 634-6659
tpc@execpc.com
www.tpclaw.com

Ronald Fatoullah, Esq.
Ronald Fatoullah & Associates
60 Cutter Mill Road, Suite 507
Great Neck, NY 11021
(516) 466-4422
rfatoullah@fatoullahlaw.com
www.elderlaw-newyork.com

Kelly G. Frére, Esq.
Matthew B. Frére, Esq.
Guyton & Frére
1001 E. Broadway
Lenoir City, TN 37771
(865) 694-0373
kfrere@gfelderlaw.com
mfrere@gfelderlaw.com
www.gfelderlaw.com

William L. Hubbard, Esq.
Hubbard & Kurtz, LLP
1718 Walnut Street
Kansas City, MO 64108
(816) 467-1777
whubbard@mokanlaw.com
www.mokanlaw.com

Sanford J. Mall, Esq.
Mall Malisow & Cooney, PC
30445 Northwestern Hwy.,
Suite 310
Farmington Hills, MI 48334
(248) 538-1800
sjmjd@teclf.com
www.theeldercarelawfirm.com

Harry S. Margolis, Esq.
Margolis & Bloom, LLP
535 Boylston Street, 8th Floor
Boston, MA 02116
(617) 267-9700
hsm@margolis.com
www.margolis.com

Sharon Rivenson Mark, Esq.
Law Office of
Sharon Rivenson Mark, PC
855 Summit Avenue
Jersey City, NJ 07307
(201) 239-0300
srm@rivensonmark.com
www.rivensonmark.com

Leonard E. Mondschein, Esq.
The Elder Law Center of
Mondschein and Mondschein, P.A.
10691 North Kendall Drive,
Suite 205
Miami, FL 33176
(305) 274-0955
lenlaw1@aol.com
www.miamieldercarelawyers.com

Cynthia R. Pollock, Esq.
Law Offices of Cynthia R. Pollock
109 West Torrance Boulevard,
Pier Plaza, Suite 101
Redondo Beach, CA 90277
(877) 849-8916
cynthia@cynthiapollock.com
www. cynthiapollock.com

Vincent J. Russo, Esq.
Vincent J. Russo & Associates, P.C.
1600 Stewart Avenue
Westbury, NY 11590
(516) 683-1717
vincent@vjrussolaw.com
www. vjrussolaw.com

Howard Krooks, Esp.
Elder Law Associates, P.A.
7284 W. Palmetto Park Road
Suite 101
Boca Raton, FL 33433
(561) 750-3850 or (800) ELDERLAW
hkrooks@elderlawassociates.com
www. elderlawassociates.com

Index

Acknowledgments

JUDITH GRIMALDI

I want to especially thank Pierre Lehu and Joanne Seminara, who captured my imagination with the concept of 5@55. Together we developed the 5@55 public education campaign and wrote this book. I thank my clients who generously shared their stories, which added so much to this book. I also acknowledge Margaret Coppola, Kim Major, and Natalie Babb, who helped me with organizing my notes and materials and helpe spread the word about 5@55. I thank my law partner, Pauline Yeung-Ha, who supported me, shared ideas, and was always enthusiastic for the project. Most importantly, I thank Neil Cohen, my life partner, who gave up weekends while I wrote, who read galleys, critiqued book covers, and encouraged me throughout the process. It was a learning experience to create a concept and a supporting campaign and book, and to work in a truly collaborative way on an effort that will help individuals age successfully.

JOANNE SEMINARA

To my family: first and foremost, my loving husband and co-author, Pierre A. Lehu, who supports me in all ways; my son, Peter J. Lehu, and daughter-in-law, Dr. Melissa Sullivan; my daughter, Gabrielle L. Frawley and son-in-law, James J. Frawley; my parents, Anita Seminara and Joseph F. Seminara, Esq., who continue to inspire me; my sister, Juliette Campasano; my brothers, Joseph F. Seminara, Jr. and Frank P. Seminara; my beautiful grandson, Jude Sullivan Lehu. I want to thank my dear friend and esteemed elder law pioneer, co-author Judith D. Grimaldi, Esq., who by her tireless advocacy and service to our profession improves the lives of older adults every day; talented colleague Pauline Yeung- Ha, Esq.; esteemed Former Surrogate Judge of New York County, Professor, and CUNY Law School Dean Emerita, Kristen Booth Glen, for her most gracious contribution of the fesewordto our book; Dr. Ruth K. Westheimer for her "joie de vivre," and our publisher, Kent Sorsky of Quill Driver Books, who steadfastly and patiently supported the creation of this book from start to finish!

About the Authors

 **Judith D. Grimaldi** is a partner in the pioneering elder law firm Grimaldi & Yeung LLP. A Certified Elder Law Attorney, Grimaldi represents the rights of the elderly and disabled, and she has special expertise on Medicare, Medicaid, health law, trusts, and wills and estates. In addition to her more than twenty years' experience as an attorney, Grimaldi has more than a decade of field experience as a social worker, which has given her a unique, first-hand perspective on the day-to-day impact of aging and disability. A 1993 graduate of Brooklyn Law School, Grimaldi also holds an MSW from Hunter College of the City of New York (1982, with honors) and a BA from Marymount Manhattan College with a certificate in Gerontology (1980, summa cum laude).

 **Joanne Seminara** has been an attorney licensed to practice law in New York and New Jersey for almost three decades. Seminara practices in the areas of elder law, estate and trust planning, including estate tax and Medicaid planning, and special needs planning. She is of counsel to the elder law firm of Grimaldi & Yeung LLP. An attorney known for her thoroughness, tenacity and compassion, Seminara has experience in many other areas of practice, including residential and commercial real estate, corporate law, employment law, and land use and zoning matters.

Pierre A. Lehu has a decades-long career as a publicist, agent, and writer. He has written over twenty books, including *Sex for Dummies*, *Sake: Water from Heaven*, *Fashion for Dummies*, and *Living on Your Own*.